Praise for **The Set-Up**

"What Simone Fulmer Gaus has done for law firms mirrors what I've seen across all businesses: Clarity beats overwhelm, and *The Set-Up* shows you exactly how to get there."
MIKE MICHALOWICZ, author of *Profit First* and *The Money Habit*

"This book is a gift to every lawyer drowning in the chaos of running a law firm. Simone Fulmer Gaus didn't just survive the struggle—she studied it, solved it, and turned the solution into a system that anyone can apply. Her insights are refreshingly real and immediately useful, and her content is thorough and balanced. If you want your firm to shift from constant firefighting to consistent, structured growth, read this book. It will open your eyes and give you actionable steps to take it to new levels."
JOE FRIED, founding partner of Fried Goldberg LLC and founder of the Academy of Truck Accident Attorneys (AATA)

"Today is the day to read *The Set-Up*. Simone Fulmer Gaus delivers uncanny clarity on the pain points we all encounter and provides a proven, practical structure for creating your firm's ideal operations. I took pages of notes and immediately started implementing changes. I only wish I'd had this resource years ago."
SUSAN CARNS CURTISS, CEO of Girl Attorney LLC

the set-up

Build What Matters. Fix What's Broken. *Finally* Make Your Law Firm Work.

Simone Fulmer Gaus

the set-up

PAGE TWO

Some names and identifying details have been changed to protect the privacy of individuals.

Cataloguing in publication information is available from Library and Archives Canada.

ISBN 978-1-77458-693-8 (paperback)
ISBN 978-1-77458-694-5 (ebook)

Page Two
pagetwo.com

Cover, interior design, and illustrations by Fiona Lee

theset-up.co

To my FG team—Those who bought in from the beginning,
those who made us better along the way,
and those who'll take it further than I ever could.
Thank you for choosing what works over what wows,
for staying grounded in what matters,
and for building something real.
You knew it before I did:
sometimes you've got to give up sexy.
That choice made all the difference.
This is yours.

Contents

A Note from the Author

I HAVE THIS FRIEND, Jeff. He's a golfer extraordinaire. I'm more of a cart driver myself, club special in hand, enjoying the gorgeous view. But Jeff's the real deal. Zen, focused, always trying to get better.

For the longest time, Jeff had a little glitch in his swing with a big impact on his game. It was a sharp and stubborn slice, always curving hard to the right.

He tried everything: fancy coaches, magic clubs, secret YouTube gurus. He read articles. Did the drills. Bought the things. Still, nothing worked. The ball just kept veering off, like it had better plans for the weekend.

Then one day, he's at this public course where the grass is more of a suggestion than a surface, and his buddy says, "Hey, that guy over there? That's Cal. He's a legend." Cal had coached high school golf and now mostly stood around watching in that quiet, wise way people get when they've been paying attention for a long time.

So, Jeff walks over, takes a few swings, and asks if Cal has any advice. Cal nods once and says, very calmly:

"Put your elbow in your pocket."

That's it. That's the whole lesson.

And because life is weird and grace sometimes shows up in strange clothing, Jeff tries it, and *boom*. The slice is gone. Straight shot. Again. And again.

Later, Jeff told me, "It's not like I hadn't heard that kind of advice before. It just . . . landed, you know? Something about the way he said it."

I've thought about that moment a lot. How the right words, said at the right time, can change everything.

That's what this book hopes to be for you. An elbow in your pocket. A new way to see your firm, and just maybe a new way to see yourself within it.

Some of what you'll read may sound familiar, but this time, it might finally connect. Other parts might challenge long-held beliefs about how a law firm *has* to run. That's intentional. Because when you've been too busy for too long, it's easy to stop questioning what no longer makes sense.

So, take a breath. Look around. This is your invitation to reimagine what's possible. For your firm. And for you.

(Also, please hydrate. And stretch. And take a nap if you need one. That's not in the book, but it's still good advice.)

Welcome. Truly. I'm so glad you're here.

SIMONE FULMER GAUS

June 17, 2025

Prologue

"WE NEED A PLAN B."

Harrison's words cut through the heavy silence of the small conference room. Each syllable landed like a punch in the gut.

I froze, my hands tightening around the edge of the conference table.

"What are you talking about?" I asked, my voice steadier than I felt.

But I knew. *Of course*, I knew.

The truth had been gnawing at me for months, sinking its teeth in deeper with every unpaid invoice and every sleepless night.

"I just talked to the bookkeeper." Harrison exhaled, pinching the bridge of his nose. "We don't have enough to cover next month's payroll. We can't keep this up, Simone. We're not gonna make it."

And there it was.

A wave of nausea rolled through me as his words hung in the air. I wanted to argue, to tell him we'd figure it all out. But the truth hit hard.

It was June of 2016, and our law firm had been in business for just over a year and a half. On the surface, we were doing everything right. We had clients. We were doing good work.

But behind the scenes, our dream of success seemed to be fading away. No matter how hard we tried, the numbers just weren't adding up.

In our first year, we had one major settlement that covered our overhead for about six months. Our office space—an ambitious effort at creating an open and collaborative environment—cost almost all of my savings for the build-out, furniture, and equipment. The rent alone was staggering. And on top of all that, each case we handled was costing upward of $50,000 in expert fees and deposition costs.

We were drowning.

A line of credit carried us through when fees weren't coming. But it was maxed out from paying overhead and salaries to two paralegals, two legal assistants, and two lawyers other than Harrison, my partner, and me. Neither of us had yet taken home a penny.

This wasn't the dream. Not even close. This wasn't the firm I'd imagined when I drained my savings to build it. It felt like I had built something *beautiful*—something I *believed in*—only to watch as it crumbled in my hands.

Harrison hesitated, waiting for me to say something. When I didn't, he gave me one last look before walking out. He softly closed the door behind him.

And just like that, the fragile threads holding me together began to unravel. Shame rose, hot in my throat.

This wasn't just a law firm. It was my reputation and my future. And these people—our team—left behind jobs and security to join me. They believed in me. They trusted me.

But I didn't have a plan B. I don't believe in plan Bs.

Still, I knew Harrison was right. Something had to change.

And it was there in that empty room, with nothing left but fear—and just the faintest hint of stubborn hope—that a voice inside me pushed through the doubt: "You wanted to do things differently. You wanted to change the way lawyers think about and practice law."

And that's all I needed.

Because when there's no plan B, you damn well better make plan A work.

1

It Wasn't Supposed to Be This Hard

Unless someone like you cares a whole awful lot, nothing is going to get better. It's not.
DR. SEUSS, *The Lorax*

NO. YOU'RE NOT WRONG.

Running a law firm is hard. *Really* hard. You're wrestling with the day-to-day demands of managing the firm, the constant push to bring in clients and keep the ones you have, and, as Harrison reminded me, the unrelenting pressure to actually make money.

You probably started your firm with a clear vision. You knew exactly what you wanted it to be. But somewhere along the way, something changed. The demands piled up and the urgent overtook the important. You found yourself constantly pulled in different directions, fighting fires, answering questions, and solving problems only you seemed able to fix.

Maybe you don't have the culture you want; people keep leaving, and the ones who stay don't act like they want to be there. Maybe case outcomes are disappointing. Or delegation feels too risky because, if you step back (or even dare to), can you really trust things to get done the right way?

It wears on you. Your days blur together, deadlines pressing in, problems multiplying. And somehow, despite all the effort, things still go sideways. Then at night, sleep won't come. You lie there, staring at the ceiling, wondering how to fix it all and maybe questioning why you even try anymore.

Sometimes (more often than you might like to admit), you feel out of control. Like you don't know where to focus. Or worse, you're not even sure where to start.

I've been there.

I know how these issues can stretch your days thin and leave you wondering how to make it all work. I know the exhaustion of juggling more than seems humanly possible. And like you, I've learned that owning a law firm is about so much more than practicing law. It's about managing a business—a business with complexities law school never prepared us for—with every day bringing a new, frustrating challenge.

And while none of us go into business expecting to fail, the tough truth is most businesses do. According to the US Bureau of Labor Statistics, about 20 percent of new businesses don't make it past the first two years. By the five-year mark, nearly half will have closed their doors. Only 35 percent get to ten years, and then just a quarter survive to fifteen years or more.

Think about that. Fifteen years in, and only one out of four is still standing. It's heartbreaking.

But there is hope!

It is widely recognized that those business owners who survive—the ones who build something that lasts—aren't just making it up as they go. They create a plan, execute it, and keep nurturing it over time. (Reality check: I'm not sure who needs to hear this, but we aren't just lawyers with a firm, *we* are business owners, too.)

And if we go back to that day in June of 2016, when Harrison shattered my illusion of our perfect firm, a plan's exactly what *we* needed.

Sure, he'd asked about a plan B. But we really didn't have a plan A—unless you count "open a law firm and run it the way you've always seen it done." A handful of lawyers, each handling their own caseload in their own way, giving instructions on the fly, and doling out money like a sailor on shore leave—with no budget, no runway, no idea when the next fee would hit.

In that moment, though, all I could really focus on was getting through our immediate money woes. If you're wondering how we did it, well, it was a small loan from my dad. Embarrassing and hard? You bet. I was forty-eight years old, running home to Daddy crying for money. But we made payroll.

Still, fixing an immediate challenge wasn't going to solve everything. We had operational battles to fight and team issues to sort out. And we wanted to grow. What we needed wasn't just another temporary workaround. We needed a plan. An actual strategy to make sure we didn't end up as yet another statistic in the Labor Department's files.

But what were we going to do?

Figuring It Out

I don't have an MBA. Back before I decided to go to law school, my college roommate, LeAnn, suggested I go in that direction because she had and was making nearly four times what I was as a music teacher. Tempting? Of course. Who doesn't want to make more money? But business? Boring!

Yet, twenty-five years later, when I first started as a business owner, each day felt like I was hanging on by my fingernails. And my toenails. And whatever else I could muster.

There I was, tossing and turning at night, fretting about money, worrying if we'd have enough to cover both next month's utility bill *and* the invoice for a vital expert. Or, whether we'd get paid on a recent settlement before the rent came due.

During the day, my mind would race with all the "shouldn't wes." Shouldn't we have more cases lined up? Shouldn't we be doing more to market? Shouldn't we be trying that new trial software? Shouldn't we, shouldn't we, shouldn't we.

And just when I'd finally get my mind calmed down from all that second-guessing, the copier would break down, or I'd be pulled into a spat between team members, or someone would come to me with a problem on a case. Every time I turned around, there was something new demanding my attention.

Of course, all the while, I was trying to practice law according to the high standards I'd always set for myself. I kept convincing myself (or should I say "lying"?) that only *I* could deliver on the promises made to our clients and referring lawyers. After all, *I* was the one with the most experience, the one with the reputation. If *I* wasn't personally involved in every case, something would inevitably go wrong.

Should I have taken LeAnn's advice?

But then one (glorious!) day, an angel in the form of my friend Rick Hadrava threw me a lifeline. He invited me to join his mastermind group.

I almost said no. I mean, could I really take half a day out of the office? What if something went wrong while I was gone? *They need me!* Thankfully, Rick convinced me, and those few hours every month turned out to be exactly what I needed.

The mastermind meetings gave me a space where I could step back, breathe, and gain a little perspective. And no, this wasn't one of those things where a bunch of lawyers swap war stories. Instead, it was a CPA, an insurance agent, a couple of old home renovators. Each brought unique insights I would never have encountered if I'd stayed stuck in the same old law firm bubble.

One of the first things they taught me was the impact of carving out dedicated time for firm business. The idea was simple: If I spent just 10 percent of my workweek focused solely on the business, I'd gain clarity.

So, despite my initial reluctance to spend time away from handling cases or triaging the latest crisis, I decided to try it. Every Friday morning, I locked myself away to brainstorm and think about the firm. I scrutinized our numbers and strategized new ways to bring in business. I dreamed up ways to motivate the team. I pored through more business books and magazine articles than I can count.

Then Monday morning, I'd return to the office ready to try something new with the rest of the team. Some things worked. Some didn't. But within about six months of this focused approach, I began to see improvement. Not just in my sanity, but in the whole operation.

We build our firms by copying what we've seen. But that system wasn't built for modern practice—and it's failing us.

Now don't get me wrong. It wasn't like there were these immediate, big whopping changes. Progress came in inches, with little improvements, one after another. (Think about it. Isn't that how *real* change often works?)

And over time, a pattern started to emerge. Nearly everything we were doing to run the firm fell within one of five areas: People, Pipeline, Process, Product, and Profitability—what we started calling "pillars."

I found the more we focused on these pillars, the easier it became to manage that "everything, everywhere, all at once" feeling of running the firm. For the first time, things were moving forward—almost automatically—without me constantly pushing. I wasn't chasing every loose end or looking over everyone's shoulder. I finally had the confidence—and the bandwidth—to step back and actually lead.

And with that new capacity, I was able to reflect on our early struggles. What had held us back during those first few years? It wasn't the skill of our lawyers or the experience of our team. Both were solid. It wasn't a lack of clients or courtroom success. We had that, too.

What had really been holding us back was the system we were following: the traditional law firm model.

What do I mean by that?

I mean the structure passed down from the Middle Ages, born out of the old guild system, where knowledge, control, and authority sit with the "master," and everyone else just follows orders. Today, that role falls to the senior lawyer or firm owner. Information flows top-down. Work gets assigned based on rank, not skill. Most of the team doesn't see the big picture; they're left out of it entirely.

And the truth is, most of us build our firms by copying what we've seen. That top-heavy, reactive model is what we think law firms are supposed to look like. It's no one's fault. We're taught to follow precedent, after all, so that's what we do.

The problem is that system wasn't built to run a modern law firm. And it sure wasn't built to last.

But once we started building the firm around the five pillars—working them, testing them, refining them—things changed. The team knew exactly what to do and who owned it. The cases and the business ran more smoothly. We had a handle on our money. We enjoyed more of what we were doing. We had more time to *actually live*.

And it all came down to one thing: a simple system based on five powerful pillars.

Yes, it was different. And no, it wasn't the same old way of doing things.

But it was working.

And I was about to learn that it was so much more.

During our firm's third or fourth year, I was at another mastermind meeting with Rick and the gang. This time, Rick was guiding us through the process of creating strategic business plans for the year ahead.

"This isn't just a list of goals for the year," he explained. "A real business plan pulls your team together, keeps your clients engaged, guides your growth, and keeps your finances on track. It's what gives your business direction and the strength to keep going long term."

I almost laughed out loud. Without realizing it, we already had a strategic business plan; we just hadn't called it that. Everything we'd been doing—organizing the firm around the five pillars—was exactly what Rick was describing. We *did* have a plan. Take that, Labor Department statistics!

We call our plan The Set-Up. And, yes, I know it might sound a bit gimmicky at first. (But the alternative? The 5 Ps? I mean, *ugh!*)

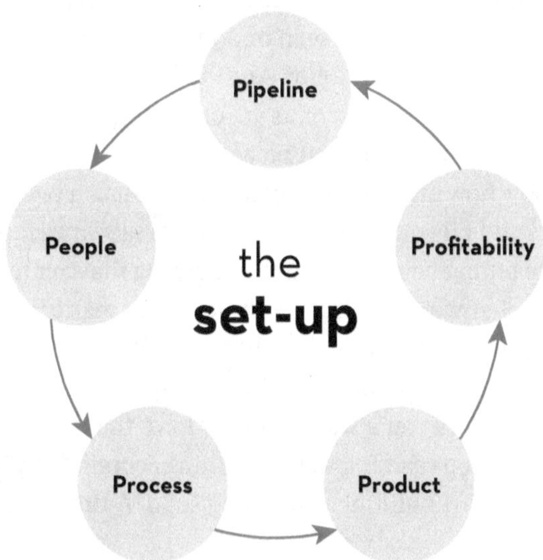

Seriously though, we chose this name for a reason. The Set-Up keeps us focused on what actually matters—building and maintaining a strong foundation to ensure the long-term success of the firm.

And the results speak for themselves.

What was once a chaotic, reactive, cash-strapped law firm is now a streamlined, profitable, and meaningful business. Eleven years in, our revenue has soared 1,200 percent—that's *thirteen times* over. And it's still growing. But best of all: We've built all this without losing ourselves in the process.

Turns out, I didn't need an MBA after all!

Let's Get You Set Up

You've poured so much of yourself into your firm: your time, your talent, your energy, your heart. You've held everything up through long nights, tight deadlines, tough calls, and impossible choices. You've given it all you've got.

Now it's time for the business you've built to start giving something back.

To get there, I'm going to ask you to make a change, to reimagine what your firm could be. To get curious. To explore doing things differently than you've likely seen or done before. That means reconstructing your foundation a bit. And, yes, it will take some work. Because the truth is too many of us are operating inside a system that was never built for us in the first place.

And I know how unsettling change can feel. It can twist your stomach in knots and fill you with doubt. But that resistance might just be fear's way of telling you you're onto something that matters.

Because what we're talking about here *does* matter. You deserve to have a law firm that genuinely delivers on all the blood, sweat, and sobs you've given it. And there *is* a better way.

The Set-Up gives you a way to finally have that firm you've been longing for. To stop reacting to all the things coming at you from all directions and start building something solid. A firm that's easier to run. One with structure, clarity, and enough calm in the middle of the storm to do great work. That's my goal in sharing The Set-Up with you, to help you build a firm that's built to sustain itself, and in the process, sustain you.

Because when you get the foundation right, everything changes:

- Your firm runs like a well-oiled machine.
- Your clients become raving fans.
- Your team steps up because they actually know how to.
- Growth stops feeling like a gamble.
- Money stops being a mystery.
- You stop bracing for impact.

And once The Set-Up is in place, even when things go a little off (and they will), you'll know exactly where to return: the foundation. That's what great performers do. Athletes, musicians, even elite military units. When the pressure's on, they rely on the basics they've mastered. Just ask Michael Jordan. Or Yo-Yo Ma. Or Demi Moore in *G.I. Jane*, training like hell to prove she belonged in the most elite military unit on earth.

If you're in the early stages of starting your firm—figuring out your business structure, shopping for printers, googling how Interest on Lawyers Trust Accounts (IOLTAs) work, and all the rest—congratulations! You've already taken a bold and important step. And, yes, you'll want these things squared away so your firm is ready for the kind of structure The Set-Up is here to give. That's where the book picks up.

So, before we get to the good stuff, take a look at the short list of essentials in *The Set-Up Workbook for Law Firms: Build It. Fix It. Make It Work.* to make sure you're ready to go. (And keep it handy as we go through the book. It's packed full of step-by-step prompts, checklists, examples, and space to build your entire Set-Up.)

For those of you who've been in business for a while and still feel like everything relies too heavily on you or is out of control, The Set-Up is for you, too.

It's time for the business you built to start giving something back.

Because wherever you are on your journey—just starting out or years in—this book isn't about just grinding it out or adding more to your already-full plate. It's about stepping back, getting clear, and finally giving your firm the structure it needs to stand on its own. Because you didn't start your firm to struggle. You built it to succeed.

And success starts with getting the foundation right.

Set-Up Focus

When I first started writing this book, one thing I kept coming back to was this: I didn't want it to be another dry, stale business book. That's not me. And you've probably read enough of those anyway.

So, at the end of each chapter, you'll find a Set-Up Focus. These won't be your typical end of chapter recaps; they're something more. Sometimes they're a story, sometimes a pause, sometimes a shift in perspective. Always, they're a space to consider not just what you're building, but how it *feels* to build it.

For this one, I want you to go back to the beginning. Not of this book, but of your law firm ownership journey. Why did you choose to do it?

I wish we could sit down over a cup of coffee (or in my case, a Coke Zero) and talk all about it. That's the mother in me, relentlessly curious, full of questions, always wanting to help. But since we can't, I'll just ask you to be honest with yourself for a moment: Why did you start? Why do you keep going?

It all started with a spark, a flash of... *something*. Just a nebulous little ember that reached that place in someone's brain where it fired the neurons and synapses into formulating a full-fledged idea. A vision. And from that vision, with a decisive stroke of action, a law firm was born.

Maybe it was your own vision or one shared with partners. Maybe it was someone else's vision you're now responsible for. Yet sometimes, you struggle with doubts. The reality of running the firm doesn't quite match the idealized vision.

When times like these come, remember that initial spark, the excitement, the sense of purpose it brought. It's still there, buried beneath the day-to-day of it all. Don't ever lose that vision and passion. It's the fuel for everything you do and will help you in those rough times. I'm glad I didn't.

But I've learned through some very tough lessons that passion alone isn't nearly enough. It gets you going, sure. But it won't keep the lights on. Only having a plan, implementing it, and sticking to it will keep the firm alive.

So, give it some thought. Don't you think it's time you had the thriving, meaningful, and profitable firm you deserve?

2

Shifting Perspective

Change. But start slowly, because direction is more important than speed.
EDSON MARQUES, *Mude*

IF THE TRADITIONAL, hierarchical way of running a law firm is one of the biggest things holding law firms back (and it is), here's the other: chasing tactics.

Take Alice, a criminal defense lawyer in Arizona, who was part of a mastermind I co-led. One day, Alice joined our Zoom meeting full of excitement. They were setting up a Slack account for her small firm.

"It's exactly what I've been wanting!" she gushed. "Since I'm out of the office a lot, going to court and taking depositions, Slack will make my life so much easier. I can keep up with all the firm talk in a single app, and everyone can ask questions and share case updates. The app even categorizes our conversations by client!"

Sounds like a great idea, doesn't it? We cheered her on.

A couple of months later, Alice returned to our meeting, but this time, without her usual contagious energy. "What's up, Alice? You seem down," someone asked.

"You're right." She sighed. She'd recently suffered a trial loss that resulted in prison time for her client. Trying to lift her spirits, someone asked how Slack was working.

"Yeah, that didn't work out... Most everybody kept texting or emailing because Slack was just another thing to check. And it was impossible to keep up with all the messages, so most of us just dropped it."

Alas, the fate of the best-laid plans.

As a law firm owner or leader, you can easily fall into the quick-fix trap—just like Alice. A challenge pops up, and you react. Or you get excited about some cool new tool, try it out, and it just doesn't land with your team.

Like the time you came back from a continuing legal education (CLE) course, buzzing with ideas and ready to shake things up. But then you walked into team drama, an angry client, and opposing counsel pulling their usual stunts. Just like that, your spark was gone, and you were back to playing the firefighter. Another idea, buried in the graveyard of good intentions.

Or when the phones went quiet for a couple of weeks, so you panicked and launched a hasty marketing blitz—discounts, promos, social posts. The calls came in, sure. But they were the wrong clients. Your team ended up overwhelmed, stressed, and wondering what the hell just happened.

Ring true? Yeah, me too. And here's what I've learned.

Those ideas that didn't take off? *Tactics*. The efforts that fell short? *Tactics*. And, yes, you guessed it: Alice's attempt to adopt Slack? Yet another tactic.

Now, make no mistake, tactics matter. They help keep our firms thriving. But on their own, they're often just a short-term fix. And as I've learned to say: You can't apply a short-term fix to a long-term problem. What actually makes the difference—the thing that gives your efforts lasting impact—is a strong foundation.

You can think of it like building or remodeling a house.

Tactics are like the latest high-tech appliances you've been eyeing or the beautiful paint colors you choose for the walls. They make the house functional and attractive. But without a strong foundation, those appliances won't matter a bit because the house itself won't stand.

You might not see it immediately. But over time, a crumbling foundation is not going to get any better. Sooner or later, you'll find yourself spending more money—not only to fix that foundation but also to replace that fancy facade.

It's no different for your firm. You can spend exorbitant amounts of time and money trying to spruce things up—fixing issues here and there with this tactic or that—but without a solid foundation, you're simply building on shifting sand. And you already know how that story ends.

So how do you know if something is just a tactic or truly foundational? It's pretty simple. Just ask yourself: Is this about getting through today or building something that will still work a year from now?

That simple question—today or a year from now?—shows up in choices like these.

> Hiring someone to handle more work when things get crazy busy? Tactic.
>
> Hiring someone who fits your culture and strengthens your team? Foundational.
>
> Jumping in to fix a problem yourself (again)? Tactic.
>
> Training your team so they know how to solve it next time? Foundational.
>
> Scrambling to cover bills while waiting on the next big fee? Tactic.
>
> Building a money system that puts you in control? Foundational.

The point is, The Set-Up helps you get clear on what's worth investing in so every tactic you try supports something bigger. And because it's built on a solid foundation, The Set-Up is something you can return to, rely on, and use to guide every meaningful decision.

That's the perspective shift we're after here: Focus on the foundation. The rest will follow.

The Set-Up Basics

So, what *is* the foundation?

The five core pillars: People, Pipeline, Process, Product, and Profitability. Together, they cover everything that truly matters when it comes to running a firm well.

Try this: Step back for a moment and imagine looking at your firm from the outside. Think about each of the five pillars. Every challenge, every decision, every moving part connects to one (or more) of them. A staffing issue? That's People. A missed court deadline? Could be Pipeline or Process. A cash flow dip? Profitability or a backed-up Pipeline.

We're going to walk through each of the pillars. As we do, just observe how they currently exist in your firm. What's already working? What teeters a little? Where do you feel stretched thin, and where can you honestly say, "We're doing something right"?

That's where we begin.

People: Our Core

When most people hear "people" in relation to a business, they think hiring. HR. Getting the right folks in the right seats. And, yes, that's part of it. You need good people to do good work.

And yet, that's not what gives the People pillar its true strength.

It's about your culture, your workplace dynamic, and—more than anything—the leadership that holds it all together. It's about clear direction, shared purpose, and core values that actually guide how your firm operates day-to-day.

You can have the best systems in the world or spend more on marketing than anyone in town, but if your culture is off—if people are disengaged, uncertain, or just punching the clock—your firm will always feel like it's working against you. That kind of misalignment doesn't just cause frustration. It leads to turnover, missed opportunities, and a firm that always feels harder to run than it should.

But when the People pillar is strong, the energy shifts. The firm gains momentum and focus. There's a shared sense of purpose, and with it, a team that's more aligned and more invested... and a whole lot easier to lead.

You can't apply a short-term fix to a long-term problem.

Pipeline: Our Framework

Our businesses exist to solve clients' problems. But to do that well, we need structure. Without it, things get chaotic. People don't know what to do or who's responsible. Important details get missed and cases drag on far longer than they should. When that happens, our service to our clients suffers.

You can prevent this with a solid Pipeline.

The Pipeline flips the traditional top-heavy approach to case management on its head, helping your team actually see what's coming, know what's expected, and move cases forward without a dozen check-ins. It maps out the entire Client Journey—from the first call to the last handshake (or hug, as the case may be)—breaking it into clear stages, defining who does what and when, so your team owns the work, start to finish.

But the Pipeline is about more than just moving cases from point A to point B. It helps you know when to hire, keeps cases from stalling, and makes sure the money keeps flowing. Without it, growth feels messy and unpredictable. With it, things run smoother, and you can finally grow in a way that actually makes sense.

Process: Our Engine

If the Pipeline is the what and who of case management, Process is the *how*. It's the step-by-step flow of how your firm actually runs, not just how cases move, but the behind-the-scenes systems that keep the whole place steady and on course.

Chances are, you already have some kind of process, even if it's mostly in someone's head, changes day-to-day, or gets reinvented every time. This is about pulling those pieces out into the open and turning them into something useful. Something your team can actually follow.

Sure, there will always be one-offs—cases that don't follow the script, moments that veer off course—but those should be the exception, not the rule. Solid processes give your team a reliable default on how to do things right, so they're not starting from scratch every time. And when the unexpected does happen, they've got the structure and the confidence to handle it well.

Product: Our Service

Most firms focus all their attention on Product, and honestly, that makes sense. It's what you actually do for your clients. It's why you went to law school, why you keep up with CLEs, and why you put in all those late nights. The motions, the hearings, the negotiations, the strategy—it's the actual lawyering, the service you're here to deliver.

But I've intentionally not put Product first in The Set-Up (or in this book), because I want to emphasize its importance in a completely different way. Why? Because you can't consistently deliver a great product if everything else around it is broken.

Without People following a Pipeline run by a robust Process, you *might* be able to produce an excellent result. Occasionally. Yet, when those wins are inconsistent—dependent on who's working the case, how burned-out they are, or how many emergencies they're juggling—your Product suffers.

When the other pillars are strong, though, everything sharpens. The quality of your work becomes more consistent. Your arguments get stronger. Your attention becomes more focused. Your client experience improves.

And when you apply Process fundamentals—breaking down best practices, documenting key workflows, identifying repeatable steps—even high-level legal work becomes more efficient and teachable. That doesn't take away the art or judgment. It just gives you a better system for delivering exactly what your clients came to you for in the first place.

Profitability: Our Results

This is where so many law firm owners get stuck: they work hard, bring in cases, and still feel like the money never quite adds up.

That's not always a hustle problem. More often than not, it's a foundation problem.

You see, Profitability isn't something you can force by raising your rates, hiring a consultant, or chasing one big case. It's something that *emerges* when the conditions for it are solid. When your People are aligned. When your Pipeline moves cases forward the right way. When your Process is consistent. When your Product is focused and clear.

Focus on the foundation.

The rest will follow.

The Profitability pillar is about putting simple, useful systems around your money, so you know what's coming in, understand what it really costs to run the firm, and get clear on what's left and where it needs to go. It's about giving yourself the information you need to make smart, steady decisions about how you spend, save, and grow.

When this part is solid, you stop feeling like your firm is one emergency away from falling apart. You get room to breathe and the space to actually enjoy running your business again.

The Set-Up: Our Strategy

Now we get to the fun part. Because when you see the pillars in isolation, it's easy to think, "Yeah, let's do the Pipeline like Simone teaches," or "She's right. We need to write down our processes." And, yes, doing those things will help enormously.

But the magic of The Set-Up comes when you stop treating the pillars like separate projects and start seeing them as parts of the same whole. When they're aligned and working together, they create something far more powerful: a foundation you can trust for planning, problem-solving, and making decisions with understanding and confidence.

You see, if one pillar is off, your foundation is off. If one is weak, the others feel the strain. You can't have a great culture (People) if cases are slipping through the cracks (Pipeline) or if the way the work gets done is a mess (Process). And no matter how strong your legal skills are (Product), if the business isn't financially stable (Profitability), you'll always feel like everything's on the verge of collapse.

But when the pillars are solid and supporting one another, your firm starts to run with ease. It supports your team. It serves your clients better. It stops demanding every ounce of your energy just to keep it standing. And when everything feels tangled or off, you don't have to guess where to look. You just return to The Set-Up. That's how you stay grounded. That's how you move forward with purpose.

It all comes down to the strength of the foundation.

Let's Talk About Marketing

You might be wondering, why isn't marketing one of the pillars?

Fair question. After all, it feels like marketing is *everywhere* these days. There's a constant hum in the background: SEO, hashtags, Google rankings, brand presence, reels, ads—the works.

And, yes, clients matter. You need them. You don't have a firm without them.

But marketing is a *tactic*, not a foundation. It's the invitation, *not* the house.

The Set-Up is about building the structure that supports everything else. Leadership that actually leads. Systems that don't fall apart when someone's out sick. People who take ownership. Financials that are clear and steady.

That's what creates the kind of firm people want to hire and recommend, because the work is solid, the experience is trustworthy, and the results speak for themselves. When your foundation is strong, your marketing doesn't have to carry the whole load.

Now don't get me wrong here, marketing *does* matter. But it fits *within* the pillars, not as one of them. It's tactical, and depending on the moment, it can play a role in any pillar: supporting your People, strengthening your Product, boosting Profitability, or helping communicate your Pipeline. Just don't confuse the megaphone with the message.

Set-Up Focus

It might seem out of place in a book about running a law firm, but there's a concept I want you to keep in mind as we move ahead: Your firm has its own DNA.

In humans, DNA is like a blueprint. It shapes everything, from the color of our eyes to our temperament and how we respond to the world around us. It's the foundation of who we are.

And just like humans, every firm has its own DNA, those internal patterns and beliefs that shape how it runs. The good news? Just like human DNA can be edited to improve health, your firm's DNA can be, too.

By creating a plan, implementing it, and sticking with it—the core principles of The Set-Up—you can rewrite your firm's DNA. You can edit what's not working and strengthen what is.

But let me be brutally honest: This. Won't. Happen. Overnight.

Anything of value takes time. It did for me, and it will for you. Anyone promising a quick fix is either lying or trying to sell you something.

And no single tactic alone can transform your firm. It's a living, breathing entity that will grow, evolve, and, yes, go through stages of entropy. The Set-Up is the foundation that holds you steady in those moments, helping you weather the strain and emerge stronger on the other side.

And the first part of that foundation? We start with the Pipeline.

I know you might expect us to begin with People. After all, that's how I introduced The Set-Up to you so far. And, yes, People are the heart, the core, of any business.

But the Pipeline is the structural backbone. Just like DNA's backbone shapes the entire strand, the Pipeline gives form and flow to your firm. It's where the work actually happens. And if that part stays messy, nothing else can truly work—not your culture, not your client experience, not your profitability.

So, the Pipeline is where we begin: your first step toward The Set-Up your firm needs.

the pipeline
our framework

IT HAPPENED SIXTEEN YEARS ago on a drive from Oklahoma City to Texarkana, Arkansas.

I was on one of those lonely Texas highways—long, straight, and impossibly empty. The road seemed to stretch on forever, and as I drove to yet another hearing, the weight on my chest grew heavier with each passing mile.

I'd been practicing law for fourteen years, the last four consumed by a single colossal battle. We were taking on the giants of the insurance industry, challenging their use of software to undervalue personal injury claims.

The fight was demanding. Relentless. And by every outward measure, incredibly successful. We had secured nearly a billion dollars in settlements; the kind of money that makes headlines and builds careers.

Yet, as I stared down that endless highway, something inside me was breaking.

I had endured the complexities of high-stakes litigation for so long, always pushing forward, never pausing to question the path I was on. The drive, the never-ending pursuit of winning, it had all become too much.

And as I drove this all-too-familiar highway, the facade I had so meticulously maintained—the one telling the world I was in control, that I had it all together—was crumbling. Bit by bit, mile by mile.

The pressure tightened, choking me from the inside. I couldn't breathe. The weight of all those years, all those expectations, was finally too much to bear. I had to pull over.

And there, in the silence of my SUV, the sobs came. Visceral. Loud. Ugly.

Later that day in the solitude of my hotel room, I came to grips with a deep truth: Despite the appearance of having it all—the big house, the fancy cars, the gold Rolex, the country club membership—I was incredibly unhappy.

I had silenced my own voice for so long, hiding behind a mask of competence and control, I'd lost touch with who I was and what truly mattered. I told myself I was doing it for my family, for our future, but the truth was harder to face.

The year my son turned two and my daughter five, I'd been away from home for thirty-eight nights. Thirty-eight missed bedtimes. Thirty-eight mornings I wasn't there. By chasing a path I hadn't truly chosen—one quietly shaped by the expectations of others—I wasn't just abandoning myself. I was abandoning them, too.

At the time, I thought I was the problem. That I just wasn't cut out for this lawyer life. That maybe I lacked the stamina, the edge, the ability to thrive in such a world. But I did what I had always done. I pushed through and I kept going.

Still, that day on the highway cracked something open in me.

I began to see it wasn't just me. It was everywhere: the pressure, the exhaustion. The burnout I had blamed on myself was actually baked into the traditional law firm model I'd spent my entire career inside. The system wasn't just failing me; it was suffocating everyone. Lawyers running on fumes. Staff burned out or checked out. Firms held together by sheer force of will.

The hustle wasn't just encouraged; it was glorified. Burnout wasn't seen as a warning sign; it was applauded as commitment. And success was measured in late nights, ever-growing case settlements, and how much you could carry before you collapsed.

But if not this, then what?

Eventually, I answered that question by doing the scariest thing I could imagine. I walked away. I left the traditional law firm I'd built my career inside to try something a little different—my own firm, created on my own terms. Because I knew if I stayed in that system one day longer, it would hollow me out completely.

And from that blank slate, I began building something different. Something that could actually support the people inside it. And the first change we made, the one that changed everything, was the Pipeline.

Not because it magically makes law firm life easier but because it gives chaos a container. Instead of cases floating in a cloud of confusion and emergencies, the Pipeline creates structure. It turns case handling into a flow. It replaces ambiguity with clarity. Panic with predictability. And it's not just about how the work gets done. It's about how people sustain themselves while doing it.

In short, the Pipeline is the best remedy for the kind of burnout breakdown I experienced on that Texas highway so long ago.

In the next few chapters, I'll show you the Pipeline, how it works, and why it makes such a difference. Not just for me, but for the team around me, for the way we show up, handle the work, and hold on to ourselves in the process.

My hope is that, as you see it in action, you'll begin to imagine what this kind of structure could mean for you, too. But more than that, I hope you see the Pipeline as a way to be more intentional with how you're doing the work. Because if the current way is costing you your peace, your energy, or your sense of self… then it's not really working.

3

A New Way to Work the Work

You wanna fly, you got to give up the shit that weighs you down.
TONI MORRISON, *Song of Solomon*

I'M FROM OKLAHOMA. And if you know anyone from Oklahoma, you know we've got a cut-to-the-chase kind of way of talking. No pretense, no fancy talk. You'll be in the middle of a conversation, and one of us Okies'll throw out something like: "We're in for a rodeo on this one," or "That's crookeder than a dog's hind leg," or "That's as useless as udders on a house." Colorful, indeed. But dead accurate.

My friend Doug's got a favorite. He's from a little town in the middle of Oklahoma. Maybe it's something folks out that way say. It was new to me.

I remember the first time I heard it. We were in the middle of strategizing a tough case, where every solution we devised caused a new problem, and tugging on one thread only made things worse. At one point, Doug leans back in his chair, laces his hands behind his head, and props one ankle over his knee. He lets out an exasperated sigh and says, "Damn! This case is just a ball of fishhooks."

A ball of fishhooks? I had to stop and really think about it.

I could see it: a tangled mass of sharp little hooks, all snagged on each other. Try to pull one free, and three more catch. Try to loosen the mess, and the whole thing cinches together. Move too fast, and it jabs you. It's messy, painful, and nearly impossible to unravel.

Now, whenever I think about the old way cases were handled, that's what I picture.

The paralegal's hovering, unsure whether to push for the draft of the motion needed to meet the filing deadline. The associate's stuck, waiting for direction no one actually said out loud. The lawyer—the only one who knows what's supposed to happen—is drowning in hearings, filings, and whatever fresh hell just landed on their desk. A client's calling again, but no one's sure who's handling the case. Everyone's just paralyzed, too unsure of who's supposed to do what and too afraid to take the initiative.

It's a ball of fishhooks.

And the question I couldn't let go of when we first started the firm: How do we actually fix this?

Birth of the Pipeline

One night, the solution finally came to me.

I was in my bedroom, the glow of my laptop lighting up the dim room as I absentmindedly scrolled through social media. It was late, but my mind was racing, turning over the same question again and again: How can we break free from the same old way of doing things?

I thought back to a trip I'd recently taken to the airport, and an idea came to me: What if we had a system like that?

Think about it. When you arrive at the airport, everything is designed to move you along: checking in, passing security, finding your gate, boarding the plane, and finally reaching your destination. Each step is part of a well-coordinated system. And when it works, it feels seamless.

Of course, airports don't always get it right. Delays happen, security lines back up, and sometimes you have to sprint to catch a flight. But that's the exception, not the rule. And that's what stuck with me. Even when things go wrong, the system's still there. It's the constant. It guides you to the next step. You don't have to wander around aimlessly hoping for a gate to mystically appear. You just follow the signs, check the screens, and adjust as needed.

That's what we needed in the firm. A way of handling cases where every step is accounted for. Where, even if something goes off track, you still know where you are and what's next.

At first, it felt like a stretch. It was such a leap from how we'd always worked. But the more I thought about it, the more it made sense.

If we could get in front of things and map out how we *wanted* cases to run, everything could become more predictable. Every client would follow the same path, even if their final destinations varied. And along the way, every team member would be prepared, knowing exactly what to do to keep things moving.

As I mulled it over, I realized some larger, high-volume personal injury firms had already taken steps in this direction. Their Intake teams were separate from the rest of the case handling. But I had never seen a firm apply that same system to more complex litigation like we handled. And I certainly hadn't seen a firm use it from the start of a litigated case to its very end. Still, I was determined to make it work. We weren't going back to the old way of handling cases!

So, I grabbed a pad of paper and wrote Client Journey at the top.

Then, I started jotting down everything that happens in a typical case. The various motions, different types of hearings, assorted filings, you name it. I also listed all the things I wished would happen without a reminder but often didn't, like sending client welcome packets, calling experts at the end of a case, or requesting Google reviews. The more I wrote, the longer the list grew, capturing all the scattered pieces in my mind.

Once I had everything down, I looked at the list. It reminded me of a heap of Legos strewn across the floor—chaotic, colorful, and

CLIENT JOURNEY TAKE CALLS ON NEW CASES **GATHER DOCUMENT**

FROM CLIENT BACKGROUND CHECK OF PL AND DEF **SET UP CASE FIL**

ORDER POLICE REPORT AND REVIEW **ORDER MEDICAL RECORDS AND BILL**

FOLLOW UP ON MEDICAL RECORDS AND BILLS (IF CLIENT CONTINUES T

TREAT) **DEVELOP CASE STRATEGY** CREATE THE NARRATIVE **INVESTIGAT**

ACCIDENT FILE PETITION/COMPLAINT **FILE MOTION TO ENTER** SCHEDULIN

ORDER **EXPERTS?** ATTORNEY-CLIENT CONTRACT **WELCOME TO THE FIR**

PACKAGE SERVE THE LAWSUIT **PREPARE DISCOVERY** RESPOND TO WRITTE

DISCOVERY **SCHEDULE DEPOSITIONS** PREPARE FOR DEPOSITIONS **G**

pipeline

THROUGH DOCUMENTS AND DECIDE ON EXHIBITS PREPARE PRETRIAL ORDE

PREPARE FOR MEDIATION PREPARE FOR TRIAL **WITNESS PREPARATIO**

NEGOTIATE LIENS, MEDICAL **KEEP CLIENTS INFORMED OF CASE STATU**

FILE PLEADINGS **ATTEND HEARINGS** SCHEDULE MEDIATION **CONDUC**

DEPOSITIONS SUMMARIZE DEPOSITIONS **ADVISE EXPERTS AND WITNESSE**

OF CASE RESOLUTION WORK ON RELEASES **ASK CLIENTS FOR GOOGL**

REVIEWS CLIENT JOURNEY **TAKE CALLS ON NEW CASES** GATHER DOCUMEN

FROM CLIENT **BACKGROUND CHECK OF PL AND DEF** SET UP CASE FI

ORDER POLICE REPORT AND REVIEW ORDER MEDICAL RECORDS AND BIL

FOLLOW UP ON MEDICAL RECORDS AND BILLS (IF CLIENT CONTINUES TO TREA

DEVELOP CASE STRATEGY **CREATE THE NARRATIVE** INVESTIGATE ACCIDE

FILE PETITION/COMPLAINT FILE MOTION TO ENTER **SCHEDULING ORD**

EXPERTS? **ATTORNEY-CLIENT CONTRACT** WELCOME TO THE FIRM PACKA

ERVE **THE LAWSUIT** PREPARE DISCOVERY **RESPOND TO WRITTEN**

ISCOVERY SCHEDULE DEPOSITIONS **PREPARE FOR DEPOSITIONS** GO

IROUGH DOCUMENTS AND DECIDE ON EXHIBITS **PREPARE PRETRIAL ORDER**

REPARE FOR MEDIATION **PREPARE FOR TRIAL** WITNESS PREPARATION

EGOTIATE LIENS, MEDICAL KEEP CLIENTS INFORMED OF CASE STATUS

LE PLEADINGS ATTEND HEARINGS **SCHEDULE MEDIATION** CONDUCT

EPOSITIONS **SUMMARIZE DEPOSITIONS** ADVISE EXPERTS AND WITNESSES

F CASE RESOLUTION **WORK ON RELEASES** ASK CLIENTS FOR GOOGLE

EVIEWS **CLIENT JOURNEY** TAKE CALLS ON NEW CASES **GATHER DOCUMENTS**

ROM CLIENT BACKGROUND CHECK OF PL AND DEF **SET UP CASE FILE**

brainstorm list

RDER POLICE REPORT AND REVIEW **ORDER MEDICAL RECORDS AND BILLS**

OLLOW UP ON MEDICAL RECORDS AND BILLS (IF CLIENT CONTINUES TO

EAT) **DEVELOP CASE STRATEGY** CREATE THE NARRATIVE **INVESTIGATE**

CCIDENT FILE PETITION/COMPLAINT **FILE MOTION TO ENTER** SCHEDULING

RDER **EXPERTS?** ATTORNEY-CLIENT CONTRACT **WELCOME TO THE FIRM**

CKAGE SERVE THE LAWSUIT **PREPARE DISCOVERY** RESPOND TO WRITTEN

SCOVERY **SCHEDULE DEPOSITIONS** PREPARE FOR DEPOSITIONS **GO**

IROUGH DOCUMENTS AND DECIDE ON EXHIBITS PREPARE PRETRIAL ORDER

REPARE FOR MEDIATION PREPARE FOR TRIAL **WITNESS PREPARATION**

EGOTIATE LIENS, MEDICAL **KEEP CLIENTS INFORMED OF CASE STATUS**

LE PLEADINGS **ATTEND HEARINGS** SCHEDULE MEDIATION **CONDUCT**

EPOSITIONS SUMMARIZE DEPOSITIONS **ADVISE EXPERTS AND WITNESSES**

overwhelming. But as I studied it, I started to see patterns. Certain pieces began snapping together, and slowly but surely, things started to take shape.

I could see that the Client Journey could be broken into distinct segments, much like the various stops in an airport. I called these "stages." Each stage covered a key milestone in the life cycle of a typical case, following a logical progression from that first call with a potential client, through building the case, pushing it forward, to reaching a resolution.

Within each stage, there were specific moves that had to happen to keep the case progressing. In other words, the actual tasks we needed to do. These became our Objectives—drawn straight from the list I'd just created. Some were the nonnegotiables we already knew had to happen in every case. Others were things I wanted to see done more consistently across the board.

And not every Objective needed to be handled by me or another lawyer. Yes, some required a lawyer's insight or skill—like brief writing and court appearances—but many could be completed by our support team: background checks, scheduling depositions, even taking the first call on new cases.

This meant we could assign Objectives based on the ability and training of team members, not just what their job title might be. We could define each team member's Role in the Pipeline based on the set of Objectives they were responsible for. All they needed to know is what the Objectives were, when each Objective was supposed to happen, and whether it fell within their Role. This way, they would know exactly what to do without someone needing to first give directions.

Then came the final piece. Most Objectives could be broken down into clear, repeatable steps—steps that could be followed the same way every time, no matter who was responsible. We could define those steps and turn them into Processes. (We'll cover these in the section on Process).

And with that, the Pipeline was born!

How the Pipeline Comes Together

The Pipeline is built by starting with the big picture (the Client Journey), then breaking it into stages, defining what must happen at each one (Objectives), assigning ownership (Roles), and finally making sure the work gets done consistently (Process).

Client Journey: the full path a case follows

Stages: the key milestones along that path

Objectives: what needs to happen in each stage

Roles: who is responsible for which Objectives

Processes: how each Objective gets done

What had started as a scribbled list I made one night while lost in Facebook became a system for working our cases—one we could rely on to keep every single case moving the way it should. It had my way of thinking, the best practices for putting a case together, built into it.

And, yes, designing the Pipeline was the easy part. The real test was putting it into action. Would it actually work in practice?

Instead of a big rollout and a showy PowerPoint presentation, I decided to just talk the team through it.

It wasn't hard for most of them to grasp the concept of Roles and Objectives. They'd done these tasks before. This was just a new way to think about them. They also understood the idea of stages. That's how a case typically moves.

What made them a little nervous was the "automatic" part, the idea that they could move cases forward without waiting for someone to tell them to. But I could see it: the excitement (and finally the permission!) to move cases on their own.

And it worked. Not overnight, but faster than one might expect.

Sample Pipeline Stages and Objectives: Personal Injury Litigation Firm

	Intake First Call → Contract Signed	Stage One Contract → Suit Filed/Settled	Stage Two Filing → Resolution/Appeal	Stage Three Resolution → Distribution	Stage Four Final Appealable Order → Resolution
Objectives	• Gather information & documents • Meet with client • Decide to accept or decline • Execute attorney-client agreement • Docket statutes of limitation • Send Client Welcome Packet	• Continue to gather evidence • Prepare petition/complaint • Prepare & send demand (80% cases) • Maintain client communication • Serve the lawsuit	• Prepare & respond to discovery • Take & defend depositions • Prepare & argue motions • Prepare for mediation & trial • Maintain client communication	• Obtain release/order of dismissal • Resolve medical liens • Distribute funds to client and counsel • Request Google review • Close case file	• File & manage appeal • Maintain client communication • Achieve successful appellate resolution

This example shows how our firm defines each stage of the Client Journey, using clear Trigger Points and Objectives that must be met before moving to the next one. While your stages and Objectives will reflect your own practice, this model gives a sense of how it all comes together.

Within a few weeks, we found our rhythm. We had a shared vocabulary. People started anticipating what was next instead of waiting to be told. The stages gave us a clear sense of where each case was and what needed to happen next. We didn't have to rely on memory or hallway conversations to keep up. For the first time, it felt like the work was carrying itself forward, without all the snags of the traditional way.

Now, over ten years in, I compare the way the Pipeline works to going through the line at Chick-Fil-A. It's fast, it's structured, and it's freakishly efficient. Every customer follows the same line, hits the same checkpoints, and ends up with exactly what they ordered because each team member knows their role and executes it to a T.

In the next section, I'll walk you through our version of the Pipeline, built around the kind of cases we handle. If you're in criminal law, estate planning, family law, or something else entirely, your stages and Objectives may look different, which is exactly how it should be.

Use this as a model. Don't worry about the details, just focus on the shape. That's what will help you build your own.

Intake

Our Client Journey begins at Intake, when we first receive a call from a potential client or referring lawyer. While there are several Objectives to accomplish during this stage, they all serve one purpose: gathering the essential information we need to decide whether we can take the case.

So why isn't Intake called Stage One? Because it happens *before* we've agreed to move forward with a potential client. Our numbered stages only begin once we've decided to commit to the client's case. Intake is simply where we carry out all of the Objectives that get us to that point.

Back in the day, Intake was all over the place. There wasn't really a system at all, just the hope that someone, somehow, would figure it out when a potential new case came in.

Let me take you back to my early days at a traditional law firm. Imagine my desk piled high with case files, papers spilling out of folders, a humming desktop in the corner, and a couple of law books shoved in for good measure. And just when I thought I couldn't possibly take on more, another file would land on top, silently demanding I make a decision.

And then it would sit.

Weeks would go by. By the time I would finally come up for air to look at it, I'd have to dig back through the file just to remember what it was even about. And once I had a decent idea about the viability of the case, I couldn't make the final call. I'd have to chase my boss down the hallway to get a yes or no. That could take months. (Seriously!) Meanwhile, potential clients were calling, anxious for an answer.

Now, with our Pipeline in place, Intake moves like a well-practiced relay team. Because everything's already been mapped out, the moment the phone rings, the support team knows exactly what to do. They simply follow the specific Objectives assigned to them. Those Objectives cover everything that makes our decision-making thorough: the right questions to ask, the documents we need to gather, and the timing to get it done.

Then, once the support staff member compiles the necessary information, the case goes straight to the lawyer responsible for making the call whether to take the case. If additional research is needed, it gets done right then and there to inform the decision. In mass tort cases, our case manager knows exactly what to look for and can make the call herself because the Pipeline gives her everything she needs.

We use a set of standards called "Case Selection Criteria" to guide these Intake decisions. These standards define what kinds of cases align with our expertise and what don't. Most of the time, that's enough to make the call right away. Outlier cases—the ones that don't neatly fit our Case Selection Criteria but might still be worth considering—are the only time I'll step in for the final say.

And, for cases outside our scope—like medical malpractice or nursing home abuse—we're upfront with clients and refer them to firms better suited for that work. This is all handled smoothly during Intake, ensuring clients get answers quickly, without dragging everything out.

The Pipeline held the entire firm together
in a way nothing else ever had.

Just Because You *Can*, Doesn't Mean You Should

You probably already know the kinds of cases your firm handles—rear-end collisions, DUIs, simple wills, maybe hostile work environment cases. But just because a potential case technically fits your practice area, doesn't mean you should take it.

You don't have unlimited resources. And taking whatever comes through the door isn't a strategy. That's how you burn out your team and fill your Pipeline with regret.

Years ago, trial lawyer Don Keenan introduced me to the concept of case selection criteria: a deliberate way to define which cases you say yes to, and just as importantly, which ones you don't.

There's real power—and honestly, a little elegance—in having clear boundaries. When everyone knows what fits and what doesn't, decisions get easier. Your team doesn't have to ask, "Are we taking this?" every other day, and Intake runs faster.

That's what Case Selection Criteria does. It defines the perimeter of your firm's work so your team can make confident decisions without needing your brain on every file.

A few things to define:

- What types of cases are a clear yes (e.g., slip and falls, first-time misdemeanors, basic estate plans)?
- What kinds of clients do you serve best?
- What case value or level of complexity makes a case worth your time?
- What counts as an outlier needing attorney review?
- What happens with the cases you don't take? Do you refer them out (and to whom) or decline them outright?

For clients we believe we can help, the next step in Intake is getting the client to sign a contract with us. We call that moment a Trigger Point, the action that officially moves a case from one stage to the next. In this case, from Intake to Stage One.

Whenever a Trigger Point is reached, a designated team member updates the case status in our case management software and advances it to the next stage. This keeps the entire team aligned and ensures nothing gets missed.

Stage One

Stage One begins as soon as we have a signed contract in hand. From there, each case follows one of two paths, depending on what we uncover during Intake: the complexity of the case, the expected value, and the likelihood of early resolution.

If it looks like a case can resolve quickly without a lawsuit, it goes into what we call the 80% track. If litigation is likely, it enters the Litigated Cases track from the start.

Our 80% cases are handled by the 80% Team, which works through a streamlined set of Objectives: ordering records, checking liens, reviewing damages, preparing the demand, and starting negotiations. If the case settles early, it moves directly to Stage Three. If it doesn't, we shift it to the Litigated Cases track and proceed from there.

Consider an 80% Approach

The idea of the 80% Team came from the Pareto principle, also known as the "80/20 rule." It suggests that 80 percent of results come from 20 percent of efforts. I used a similar idea to organize our caseload.

Back in the day, attorneys juggled everything—complex bad faith cases alongside straightforward car accidents. The smaller, faster cases made up the bulk of our work, but they constantly pulled us away from the strategic demands of high-value cases. We were stretched too thin. And no case, not even the important ones, got the attention it truly needed.

That's why we created the 80% Team: a dedicated group focused on faster-moving, lower-value cases. This freed the rest of the firm to stay focused on complex litigation, where deeper strategy and legal skills are required.

More complex Litigated Cases—like bad faith, trucking, or serious injury claims—follow a different approach and start on a more intensive track from day one. These cases require deeper legal strategy, so the paralegal begins by gathering records and organizing core documents, while the attorney drafts the Case Narrative (we'll talk more about this when we discuss Product) and does any needed research. The final Objective in Stage One for Litigated Cases is preparing and filing the petition or complaint. That filing is the Trigger Point that moves the case to Stage Two.

In either track, the key is this: Resolution or filing is what keeps the Pipeline moving forward.

Stage Two

Stage Two begins once the petition or complaint is filed, initiating the formal start of litigation. The Objectives in this stage cover everything that must happen from that point through the end of trial.

Again, let's go back to my early days at a traditionally structured firm. There, every case we handled was slated for litigation, so we knew as soon as it came in what was in store. But like many firms at the time, our "case management" was really just deadline management—especially statutes of limitations.

That is, unless a case was the "big whale" of the moment (the one consuming everyone's time and energy), cases just sat there, gathering dust. Most didn't get attention until a deadline loomed. And when that happened, I was scrambling to "keep us out of malpractice" on those back-burner cases. I'd rush to meet the deadline and then dive back into the "biggest case in the firm."

Once the big case wrapped, we'd shift gears to the next "big whale," leaving a trail of neglected cases behind. It was always the same drill: Pick one case, throw everything at it, and let the others wait. Sometimes it was the case sitting the longest. Sometimes it was whichever one screamed the loudest.

We designed Stage Two to prevent that scramble and to make sure every case keeps moving.

Most of the logistics of litigation—organizing documents, tracking deadlines, filing—are handled by our support staff, following the particular Objectives assigned to them. And because Stage Two is the most lawyer-intensive part of our Pipeline, that structure frees our lawyers to focus on what only they can do: legal strategy and execution.

But make no mistake: Our support team isn't just supporting. They're *leading*. Our litigation paralegals are the ones driving Stage Two forward. They know the Objectives in every case and make sure each one gets done. Yes, even if an Objective belongs to a lawyer, the paralegal is right there with (mostly) gentle nudges to the lawyer to keep things moving. That's why I often say, "Shelley's the boss, not me."

As a result, cases don't sit still waiting for direction. They keep moving because the people doing the work know what needs to happen next and they just do it.

Because litigation isn't linear, moving in unpredictable bursts that can stretch out for months or even years, we eventually broke Stage Two into three internal phases. These aren't separate stages. They're guideposts within the larger stage to keep us oriented and focused. You may not need phases like this, but I want to show how you can adapt the Pipeline to fit your work.

- In Phase One, we build the foundation: gathering records, sending discovery, and reinforcing the Case Narrative from Stage One.

If it matters,
make it
an Objective.

- In Phase Two, things ramp up—depositions, legal strategy, and motion practice all take center stage.
- And in Phase Three, we focus on trial prep: finalizing exhibits, scheduling witnesses, and tightening our arguments.

Breaking Stage Two down this way gives us the ability to keep track of multiple litigation-heavy cases at once. We know exactly where each case stands, what kind of attention it needs, and who's driving it forward.

Stage Three

Stage Three is triggered as soon as a case is resolved, whether that happens in Stage One or at any point in Stage Two or Four. From that moment on, the focus shifts to closing things out: lien reductions, referral payments, and final client communication.

We carved out an entire stage for case resolution because these final details matter. If they're overlooked, they can delay payment to the client and the firm. Worse, they can raise ethical issues around client funds if not handled with care.

That's why a different team member takes the lead here. They're not involved in the day-to-day of active cases, so they can give everything the attention it deserves. A lawyer steps into Stage Three as needed, usually to review release documents or help deliver the check to a well-deserving client.

And because Objectives have already been built into the Pipeline, tasks like sending thank-you notes or requesting Google reviews—those little things that matter but often get lost in the shuffle—actually happen. They're part of the plan.

On that note: If it matters, make it an Objective.

Stage Four

Appeals have a dedicated stage. They don't come up often—maybe three or four times a year—but when they do, they're high-stakes and time-sensitive. Before the Pipeline, one appeal could throw the whole team into a whirlwind. We'd scramble to figure out deadlines, dig up the rules, and pull people off other cases just to keep things from falling apart.

Now, Stage Four keeps us focused on what makes appeals different: strict timelines, distinct strategies, and procedures that don't look anything like litigation or trial. Because they're built into the Pipeline, we're ready. Even with long gaps between filings or hearings, the structure holds. We can shift gears and pick things back up without losing momentum.

And when the appeal is resolved—whether we win, lose, or get remanded—the next step is clear. If it's remanded, the case moves back to Stage Two, where the litigation team picks it up again. If we lose entirely, we take it to Stage Three for closing procedures. Either way, there's no confusion about what happens next.

Every Practice Has Its Own Flow

Wondering what a Pipeline might look like in your area of law? Here are a few example progressions.

- *Family Law:* intake → filing → temporary orders → discovery → mediation → trial or settlement → resolution
- *Criminal Defense:* intake → investigation → negotiation → trial prep → resolution or sentencing
- *Estate Planning:* consultation → document drafting → client review → signing → funding or follow-up

No matter the area, the structure underneath stays the same:

- The Client Journey defines the path
- Each stage marks a key milestone
- Each Objective moves the case forward
- Roles clarify who's responsible for what
- Processes make each step consistent and repeatable

The details may vary, but the framework gives you something to build on, so your work becomes easier to track, train, and trust.

The Set-Up Workbook for Law Firms includes sample Pipelines for different practice areas. There's also a Quick-Start Guide at the end of this chapter so you can start building your own.

Set-Up Focus

I didn't set out to build a framework. I was just trying to organize the junk drawer of my mind—the half-formed ideas, the forgotten follow-ups, the things we kept meaning to fix but never did. I thought, maybe if I could just get it out of my head and onto paper, we'd survive.

But the Pipeline turned out to be much more than a way to manage our cases. It gave us something that held every part of the firm together.

It gave our People a way to show up with confidence. Our Processes finally had a place to land and actually be used. It shaped the Product we deliver by making the work more intentional. And it supported Profitability by making results more consistent and less dependent on constant heroics.

"Sure, that all sounds great on paper, but what if I let go and my team screws it up?"

That's a valid concern, and you're not alone if that's your thought. I've taught the Pipeline to other firm owners, and that's the part where most of them get stuck, too.

But I'd encourage you to take a moment. Think about how things are right now.

Maybe things feel fine—the work gets done, more or less, and the wheels keep turning. But that's only because everything runs through you. Cases don't move until you weigh in, and your team keeps asking, "What do you want me to do next?" because they're waiting for your say-so.

That's the hallmark of a top-down model. And it begs the question: Is it really working?

Yes, there's comfort in staying involved in the thick of things. It's your name on the door, after all. You care about quality and letting go of the reins feels risky. But that instinct, while understandable, is also a trap. It keeps you in the weeds and away from the work only you can do. That's not structure. That's survival.

And you're not letting go blindly. The Pipeline embeds your standards and expectations into the system itself. Your way of working is still there, and your brain still guides the work. It's just finally out of your head and in a structure your team can actually use. And structure is where the best things come from.

That's where we're headed next.

Pipeline Quick-Start Guide

Ready to build your Pipeline? Awesome! You don't need software or spreadsheets, just a whiteboard, some markers, and a little willingness to make a mess before it all comes together.

Grab some of your people as you do this—the ones who actually do the work. When your team helps build the thing, they're more likely to trust it (and stick with it) once it's live.

Step One: Map out the Client Journey. Zoom out. What path does a case follow from first contact to final wrap-up? It might look something like this:

Marketing → First Contact → Representation Begins → Litigation → Resolution

Step Two: Brain dump the Objectives. Zoom in. What actually has to happen along that path? These are your Objectives–the real steps that move the case forward, like "send welcome packet," "order police report," "draft complaint," "schedule deposition." Write down everything. Even the little stuff. Organize it later.

Step Three: Define the stages. Group those Objectives into stages. What naturally fits together? Name a Trigger Point for each stage so it's clear when one stage ends and the next begins.

Step Four: Assign the Roles. Next to each Objective, write who's responsible. This is how you build real accountability.

Step Five: Start, watch, adjust. Try it on a real case. Then another. Watch what works. Adjust what doesn't. Your Pipeline isn't precious. It's a living system that gets stronger every time you use it.

4

What Happens When the Work Works

Life moves pretty fast. If you don't stop and look around once in a while, you could miss it.
FERRIS BUELLER, *Ferris Bueller's Day Off*

OKAY, I HEAR YOU.

Operations isn't exactly the kind of thing that gets you jumping out of bed in the morning. Just thinking about it probably makes your stomach drop. And then comes that awful bile creeping up the back of your throat. *Blech!*

Deep breaths now.

You're not alone in hating the idea. But getting a handle on your firm's case management isn't just for those "operations people" out there. It's for you, as the leader of your firm, because if you don't shape how things run, someone else will... and you may not like how that turns out.

And I get it. When it comes to doing things I don't love, I'm a pro at procrastination. Take my closet, for example. It's all mine, not shared with my husband, so I think my "system" of organizing is just fine.

My system? Let's just say if the clothes aren't on the floor, I call it a win.

But let me tell you, that "system" hasn't always made things easy. I'd get up in the morning, thinking, "I'm going to wear this outfit today." I'd go to my closet and rifle through, trying to find what I want.

Inevitably, being the clotheshorse I am—here's the idea: twenty-seven sweaters, twelve winter coats, eighty pairs of shoes—I couldn't find that one thing I had in my head. I'd get so frustrated!

Mark, my sweet husband, would just laugh at me. As a former Marine, his closet is perfect—everything lined up, arranged by type of clothing and color—and he never has trouble knowing exactly where anything is. He kept telling me how I could end my frustration, but I was so resistant!

Finally, his mocking forced me to come to terms with my "problem." So, I scheduled a Sunday afternoon to put my closet into shape. Then I started putting it off. I'd say, "Next weekend I'll do it." Then the set weekend would come, and I'd say, "No, *next weekend*." Finally, Mark agreed to help me, so I'd actually tackle the job.

Honestly, I hated every minute of it. I cursed the process the whole way through. But little by little, as I saw things coming into order, I felt a sense of calm sneaking in. It only took about two hours to do it, and at the end I wondered, "Why did I wait so freaking long to do this?"

Wouldn't you know it, something incredible happened once it was done. My mornings got easier. I could find the outfit I had in mind. And my stress dropped dramatically. You see, my little "system" had been failing me. I thought I'd been fine the whole time, but I wasn't. I was just so used to the craziness that I didn't realize how much it was slowing me down until it wasn't.

And isn't that exactly how we treat our law firm operations?

We think, "Everything's fine" or "It is what it is," even though we're constantly rifling through tasks, putting out the next fire, and getting frustrated when things don't go as planned. We convince ourselves it's normal. That we can live with it.

But we don't have to!

Just like organizing my closet made mornings easier, organizing your case management will free up your time and energy. Sure, going through the work of shifting to a Pipeline might feel like another dreaded "closet clean-out" moment. It's work, and it likely won't feel like fun. But once it's done, you'll wonder why you waited so long and swear you'll never go back. Because the Pipeline reshapes your firm at every level:

- how the work flows
- how the cash is managed
- how prepared your firm is for real growth

But before we get into all that, let's get practical: How do you actually keep track of your Pipeline, without it becoming just one more thing floating around in your head?

Tracking Your Pipeline

The Pipeline is only as strong as your ability to monitor and manage it. If it's all stored mentally, jumbled in with everything else, things will slip through the cracks. To manage cases effectively then, you need a system. A reliable, visible way to track where every case stands and what's supposed to happen next. You need a Pipeline dashboard.

Think of it like the dashboard in your car: It keeps you aware of the important things. When cases are flowing smoothly, you can relax. And when something needs attention, you'll be able to spot it quickly and act before things snowball.

That visibility doesn't just help with internal management; it also gives you confidence when a client calls out of the blue, asking for an update. With a quick glance at the dashboard, you can see exactly where things stand and give a clear, confident answer without tracking down the file or the lead attorney.

You don't need fancy software to make this work. A spreadsheet, a shared doc, a whiteboard in the war room—use whatever fits your team. The format doesn't matter as much as the function. It should clearly show

- the current stage of each case,
- the next Objective,
- who's responsible,

- when the case entered that stage,
- who's assigned to keep the dashboard updated as things change.

As we move through the next sections, I'll use the term Pipeline dashboard to describe this tracking process no matter which format you choose.

"Why Would I Need a Pipeline If I Already Have a CMS?"

It's a fair question, especially if you've already invested in case management software. And for some firms, that might seem like enough.

But your CMS is a tactic. The Pipeline is the foundation.

The Pipeline defines how your firm actually runs—how cases move, who's responsible, and what success looks like at each stage. It reflects *your* strategy, *your* operations, and *your* team. That structure doesn't come built into the software. You have to create it.

Yes, some CMS vendors claim their platforms provide a complete workflow. But even the best systems are built around someone else's assumptions about how a firm should function. And when that platform changes—or disappears altogether—you're left having to learn an entirely new system from scratch.

That's not hypothetical. When our vendor of *nine years* pulled its software, our transition to a new platform was seamless because our Pipeline already held the structure. The software was just supporting it.

When your structure depends on a tactic, it's fragile. But when it's built through your Pipeline—through your team, your decisions, and your clarity—it's durable. It adapts. And it stays with you, no matter what software you use.

That's why the Pipeline comes first. Once it's in place, your CMS becomes more powerful, because now it's running *your* system, not defining one for you.

Build the foundation first. Let the tactics follow.

How Work Flows

When we created the Pipeline, we didn't know there was a name for what we were building. We just knew we'd taken the triangle of the traditional hierarchy and flattened it out. So, instead of everything bottlenecking at the top, the work would flow based on who and what the Pipeline called for.

Turns out, there's a name for what we've built: a flat organizational structure.

Flatten It Out

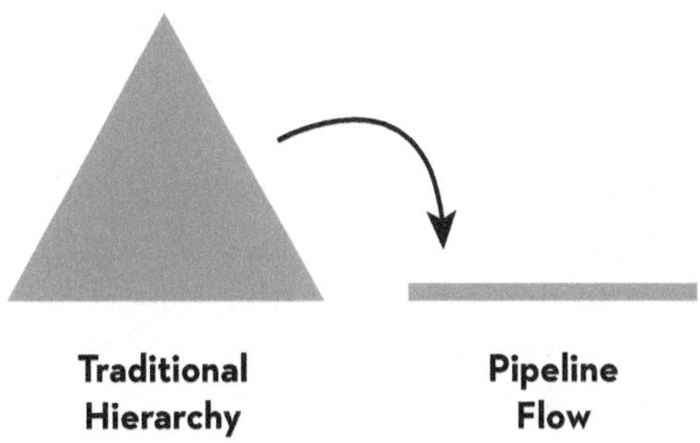

In the traditional hierarchy, everyone waits on the person at the top to decide what happens next. The Pipeline flattens that structure. It's built around the Client Journey itself, so the next step is already clear, and the team can move forward without waiting for direction.

If you've seen the television show *The Bear*, you've seen this kind of structure in action. Think about the night the restaurant reopens.

The kitchen is buzzing.

Carmy's at the pass, calling out orders, his eyes darting between tickets and plates, making sure every detail is spot on. Sydney's in the zone, plating perfectly, with quick, precise movements. At the grill, Tina flips steaks at just the right moment, while Marcus is in the back, crafting his sweet creations. Richie's everywhere all at once, reading the room, catching Carmy's nods, keeping it all moving.

Nobody's checking a to-do list or standing around waiting for instructions. Every person knows exactly where they belong and what has to happen next. You can feel the trust in the room. You can feel the momentum. The knives chopping, the burners roaring, the constant calls of "Corner!" and "Behind!" It's chaotic, sure, but it's choreographed chaos. They're all in sync.

And that's exactly what the Pipeline can bring to your firm. Not just tasks getting done, but a team that moves with purpose. Not just clearer roles, but more pride in the part they play. No more second-guessing, just a confident team doing the work, knowing what's expected and what's coming next.

We're going to start with one of the first places that clarity shows up: in how roles and responsibilities are understood inside your firm.

Roles and Responsibilities

There's this thing no one seems to want to admit about traditional law firms: They're often breeding grounds for what I call the "politics of being," that weird phenomenon where what matters isn't *what* needs to be done but *who* is doing it.

You've probably seen it, too.

A paralegal bristles at a task that feels too "secretarial." A lawyer refuses to pitch in because it's "beneath them." Everyone's guarding their turf—titles, egos, unspoken hierarchies—while the client (and the work) gets lost in the shuffle.

So, when something needs doing that's "not my job," you end up cajoling and coddling folks just to make progress. Maybe they roll their eyes, huff and puff, but do it anyway. Or maybe your go-to person just jumps in (again), because they can't stand things being left hanging.

Yep. That's what it looks like when the "politics of being" take over: inefficient, unfair, and utterly exhausting.

But with the Pipeline, everything becomes clearer. It's no longer about someone's *title*, it's about what they're *responsible for*: "These are my Objectives, and I'm carrying them out when the time comes."

And the payoff is huge. Research shows that when people have clear insight into their roles, efficiency jumps by 53 percent, effectiveness increases by 27 percent, and overall performance climbs by 25 percent. Best of all, 75 percent of people with high role clarity say they're happier at work and actually *enjoy* what they're doing.

Why wouldn't we lean into a system that delivers like that?

The thing about a Pipeline-driven mindset is that it opens the door for leadership at every level. Everyone owns what they're responsible for, and that ownership breeds accountability, confidence, and initiative, three things that get crushed in a top-down model.

We reinforce this mindset with a simple saying: "Stay in your lane." It's a reminder to stay focused on what you own and trust others to do the same. When everyone knows *what's theirs to do*, and just as importantly, *what's not*, the system flows more fluidly.

To help our team make this shift, we created a simple team exercise we call the "whiteboard exercise."

I drew the Pipeline on the board—just the stages—and asked each person to write their name where they held responsibility. (Don't worry if yours isn't beautiful, mine sure wasn't!) Then, each person added the Objectives they owned within those stages.

Yes, there was overlap. "That's expected," I explained. "A paralegal and a lawyer might both show up in Stage Two, just handling different pieces. That's fine, as long as you're clear about who owns what."

When everyone saw how the work connected, it changed the way they saw their roles. Titles lost their meaning, and ownership took over instead. People pulled out their phones to take pictures of the board. They finally had something to point to—a structure that made sense.

We still return to the whiteboard exercise. It's our go-to when things feel out of sorts, when someone hesitates, when roles blur, or when we bring on someone new. It re-centers the team on what matters: the work, the client, and the next Objective.

Identifying Bottlenecks

Remember that *I Love Lucy* episode where Lucy and Ethel take jobs at a candy factory? Okay, I know, it's from way back (even before my time!). But it's a classic, and if you've seen it, you might know exactly where this is going.

If you don't shape how things run, someone else will... and you may not like how that turns out.

At first, things are great. The belt moves slowly, the chocolates are spaced out, and Lucy and Ethel are feeling pretty good about themselves. They're standing there in their cute little uniforms, side by side, ready to take on their new job: wrap each chocolate as it comes down the conveyor belt. Easy-peasy, right?

Then the belt speeds up. Just a little.

They shoot each other a look—"We can handle this"—and start wrapping faster.

But then it speeds up again.

And suddenly the chocolates are coming down the line like a runaway freight train. Lucy's grabbing at thin air. Ethel's fumbling, missing more than she wraps. The chocolates start piling up, and panic sets in. Lucy starts stuffing them into her hat and blouse. Ethel crams them into her mouth just to keep the belt clear. Chocolates are flying. Lucy's cheeks are bulging. Ethel's panicking. Chocolates everywhere.

Total bottleneck. Complete meltdown. And all you can do is laugh, because there's no way they're getting out of this one without hearing Ricky Ricardo groan, "Oh, Luuucy!"

That's pretty much how bottlenecks sneak up on you in a busy law firm, too.

And here's where your Pipeline acts like your very own candy-factory alarm system. Instead of managing by memory or gut feeling, you can *see* where things are getting jammed in real time and step in before it turns into chaos.

Let's say a case has been sitting around forever with no progress. With the Pipeline, you can pull up your dashboard and quickly see how long the case has been stalled and which stage it's stuck in. Are there any missing steps or Objectives? Is someone waiting on a signature? Did a task fall through the cracks? Is someone overloaded? Whatever it is, the insight is right there. You can follow up, reassign tasks or Objectives, or step in with support as needed.

And it's not just about fixing *one* case.

The Pipeline helps you spot patterns. Maybe your Intake team is working efficiently, but cases are piling up in Stage One because documents aren't getting gathered fast enough. Without the Pipeline, that kind of backlog could sneak up on you, and diagnosing the source becomes a guessing game. But with the Pipeline, you can easily see which cases are stalling and where the holdup is. From there, you can assign additional support, re-prioritize tasks, or follow up directly to get things moving again.

The key is making this kind of visibility a regular habit. You can build Pipeline reviews into your weekly routine. In our firm, we hold a short lawyer meeting every week to just scan the dashboard, look for bottlenecks, and course-correct. It's quick, and it keeps things flowing. Because once you can see where things are stalling, you can make smarter, faster case management decisions.

Accountability

How often do you wake up in the middle of the night, convinced something's slipped through the cracks? I've been there, jerking awake, heart pounding, with that sudden, awful thought: "Is that brief due today?" "Has someone even started it?" You lie there, mind racing, unable to shake the sense you've missed something crucial. And the worst part is that you're the only one who's awake worrying about it.

Yes, the Pipeline can fix that, too, because with it, you'll have a self-managing team.

I know the idea of a team that manages itself can sound idealistic. But it's not. Research shows it's one of the most effective ways to improve how work gets done. When accountability is shared by everyone, workflows run more smoothly, there are fewer mistakes across the board, and daily stress eases.

The Pipeline naturally creates this same kind of environment. Accountability is built into every step, so the team keeps itself moving. Everyone knows what's expected and how their work affects the next person. If someone misses a step, the next person feels it immediately and speaks up. Nothing dramatic, just a quick check-in to stay on track.

Take Shelley, one of our litigation paralegals. She's responsible for gathering key documents in Stage One. When the case moves to Stage Two, Chad, a lawyer, expects everything to be ready. If something's missing, Chad follows up with Shelley to resolve it. On the flip side, if Chad forgets to log an important update, you can bet Shelley catches the delay and reminds him to keep it moving.

That kind of shared accountability keeps problems small. It keeps the Pipeline flowing, and gives you, the owner, actual peace of mind. You're not micromanaging every detail. You're trusting your team, trusting the system, and finally sleeping through the night.

Managing Cash

Let's talk about how the Pipeline changes how you think about your money.

Specifically, the not-having-enough-of-it part. The holding-your-breath-when-you-open-your-bank-app part. The I-hope-we-make-payroll part. If you've run a firm for any length of time, you've been there.

Remember that day back in June of 2016 I told you about? The one where Harrison told me we didn't have enough cash to cover next month's payroll? Yeah, that one. That moment forced me to completely rethink how we managed our money. The Pipeline became a key factor in turning things around. (*Profit First* helped, too, but more on that in chapter 15).

So how did the Pipeline help?

It connected the work in motion to the money we expected to bring in.

Every case moves through the same defined stages in our Pipeline. Because we've mapped the stages, we always know where a case stands and what's expected to happen next. Over time, we've also learned how long each stage usually takes, giving us a way to predict *when* cases are likely to resolve.

So, once a case enters the Pipeline, we assign two estimates to it:

Anticipated Value: how much we think the case will bring in.

Anticipated Settlement Date: when we think the case will resolve.

(I'm keeping this high-level here. The Set-Up workbook walks through the tactical details and gives you everything you need to build this.)

The Anticipated Value is based on the type of case, what we know so far, and our experience. It's a lot like how insurance companies set reserves—an educated estimate based on patterns we've seen before.

The Anticipated Settlement Date comes from knowing what stage the case is in. If it's early, the date is further out, based on the pace we expect. If we're close to mediation or trial, the resolution might be near. In Litigated Cases, we also refer to the scheduling order to set realistic targets. So, for a typical car accident case, we might estimate $25,000 based on similar cases, with a resolution date of 8–12 months out, depending on the current stage.

Then, as cases move through the Pipeline, we update both the value and the date as needed. If the facts shift or something causes a delay, we adjust. We aim to keep our projections conservative and useful. It's not perfect, but it sure beats guessing or hoping for the best.

All of this lives in our Pipeline dashboard. At any given time, we can look at the full caseload in the dashboard and see *what* revenue we expect and, more importantly, *when* we might expect it. This enables us to confidently make more-informed decisions.

For example, if we receive a large settlement, we don't rush into distributing funds or making big purchases. Instead, we check the Pipeline dashboard, which shows projected revenue over the next month, quarter, or even further.

If the next major case is six months out and the expected revenue in the meantime won't cover payroll or overhead, we hold back what we need to avoid scrambling later. But if the months ahead look strong, we know what we can invest in, whether that's hiring, growth, or other opportunities. And when the dashboard shows lighter quarters ahead, that's our early signal to ramp up marketing or revisit referral sources.

Having visibility into when we can expect revenue has also significantly eased working with the bank. If you've ever tried to explain a contingency fee model to a traditional bank, you know it can be tricky. Now, we don't try to explain, we just pull a report from the dashboard that lays out Anticipated Values and timelines. This satisfies the bank's underwriting needs and has helped us secure better terms, avoiding the higher-interest loans that non-traditional lenders offer.

While the Pipeline has been critical for us as a contingency fee firm, its benefits go far beyond that model.

If your firm charges flat fees or bills hourly, the same principle applies. When you track your work in motion through the Pipeline dashboard, you can anticipate your revenue at the same time. Flat fee firms can align billing with key milestones, like when a contract is signed or a case is resolved. Hourly firms can monitor which matters are active, which are stalled, and where to expect upcoming billable time.

No matter how you bill, the Pipeline gives you a clear view of what's ahead, eliminating the guesswork around what's coming next. Instead of holding your breath at the end of the month, you can see how cases are progressing in real time, giving you the power to manage your money with confidence. Once you've seen that kind of clarity, you'll never want to go back.

Managing Growth

So far, we've looked at how the Pipeline improves workflow and helps you get a better handle on your cash flow. Both are huge.

But that's not the whole story.

Running a law firm also means leading people, hiring smart, and figuring out how to grow without everything falling apart behind the scenes. That's where the cracks in the old way really start to show—guessing who's overwhelmed, hiring too late, and constantly reacting instead of planning.

Let's look at how the Pipeline helps you fix that. We're zeroing in on two of the biggest stress points in any firm: staffing and scaling. These are the areas where things can get extremely messy, but also where the right structure can change everything.

Staffing

A couple of weeks ago, I was chatting with my friend Tim. He's a law firm owner with a large support staff, but he has that one GOAT ("greatest of all time") of a paralegal, Vicky. Tim's starting to worry about Vicky. She's showing signs of burnout, and he thinks maybe they're pushing her too hard. "I can't lose her, Simone. She's the backbone of this place. If she leaves, I don't know what we'll do."

I think we've all had a "Vicky" on our teams at one point or another. They can handle anything and everything you throw at them. And they're the type who'll go above and beyond by doing things you haven't even thought of. I totally get Tim's concern.

So, I asked him, "Why do you think that's happening?"

Tim explained that, on paper, Vicky has the same number of cases as the other paralegals, but she's always got way more on her plate. Turns out her cases are more complex. She's handling all the big, messy litigation cases. Plus, because she's so good at what she does, she's the go-to when anything urgent or tricky comes up.

"I want to even out the workload," he said, "but no one else can do what Vicky does! I guess I'll have to hire more staff."

I feel bad for Tim, but you know what his problem is? They're still managing cases the traditional way. It's not just that Vicky has more cases, but the firm's entire caseload isn't balanced in a way that makes sense. And naturally, Tim thinks the solution is hiring more staff.

But not so fast; that might not be the case at all.

The problem comes down to how work gets assigned. Traditional case management tends to split cases based on who has room on their plate or which lawyer the support staff works for. It doesn't pay much attention to how complex those cases actually are.

This leaves team members managing every single part of a case, start to finish, no matter how demanding it may be. And this can result in uneven workloads, where someone like Vicky gets buried under the toughest cases, while others skate by with the less challenging ones.

What's missing is a structure that separates the work from the person, a way to assign based on what needs to be done, not just who has the capacity. What's missing is the Pipeline.

When the Pipeline does its job, you're no longer in the weeds. You're steering the business.

With the Pipeline, simpler tasks, like document gathering or basic file prep, can be handled by less experienced staff across all cases. More complex tasks, like discovery or trial prep, are assigned to your more skilled team members. This ensures that everyone works where they add the most value, preventing an unbalanced workload.

And then, when you consult your dashboard, you get real-time visibility into who's doing what—and when. If one person's name shows up in too many places or their Objectives start stacking up, you'll spot it. No more guessing if the work is evenly distributed. You can rebalance right away, either by shifting tasks or adding support.

The Pipeline also helps you spot opportunities for cross-training. When you notice bottlenecks or gaps, you can start training other team members to take on more complex Objectives. It builds depth across your team and gives people a chance to grow. So, when things get busy, or someone needs backup, others are ready to step in.

If, after rebalancing and cross-training, the team is still stretched too thin, that's your signal. Instead of reacting out of stress, you can look at the data and see exactly where the pressure points are, then make smart hiring decisions based on what the work actually demands.

And if hiring is necessary, you'll know exactly what kind of support you need and where, avoiding gut work and ensuring the new hire makes an immediate impact.

So, what did Tim do?

After our conversation, Tim decided to make some changes. He's already started rebalancing the workload using the Pipeline principles we discussed and is exploring cross-training opportunities for his team. He told me yesterday that Vicky already seems less stressed, and the rest of the team is stepping up in ways he didn't expect. That's the power of the Pipeline!

If you're unsure whether it's time to hire, start with your dashboard. The patterns will tell you more than your gut ever could.

Scaling

As your firm grows, you might be thinking about taking on more clients, expanding into new practice areas, or even opening additional offices. Growth is exciting, but it also raises the stakes. It means more clients, more complexity, and more chances for things to slip through the cracks. When you have a Pipeline, it's easier to handle any of these obstacles.

Let's go back to Carmy's kitchen in *The Bear*. When things heat up, Carmy doesn't panic or tear the kitchen apart. He adjusts on the fly, moving his team to where they're needed, keeping everything in sync.

The same applies to your firm. When more cases come in or new practice areas are added, you don't have to rework the whole system. The Pipeline helps you manage all the moving parts. If one area gets overloaded, it shows you exactly where to shift resources, whether that means reassigning Objectives, adding a new process for routine work, or bringing on new team members.

Now imagine Carmy is ready to open a second restaurant. He's not starting from scratch; he's simply replicating what already works. Sure, he needs new staff, but the systems and processes he's developed will carry over seamlessly.

The same goes for your firm. If you decide to open a new office, you don't need to reinvent anything. The Pipeline gives you a blueprint to follow. You can roll it out in a new location with confidence—same structure, same expectations, same clarity.

And with your Pipeline dashboard, you're not flying blind. You can monitor what's happening across every office, all from one place. No matter how much you grow, the dashboard gives you one clear source of truth.

Rolling Out Your Pipeline

You don't need a big rollout to get your Pipeline up and running. No team retreat or strategy summit. In fact, the simpler you start, the better.

Here's what I've seen work best:

- **Start with one new case.** Don't worry about transferring every active file right away. Just take the next new case that comes in and run it through the Pipeline—stages, Objectives, Roles—and observe how it moves. That one case will teach you a lot.

- **Bring your team in as you go.** Ask questions. Get their suggestions. Refine the system together. This isn't a top-down decree, it's something you're building as a team.
- **Use the whiteboard exercise.** Keep it visual, tangible, collaborative. It's one of the fastest ways to build clarity and buy-in.
- **Celebrate early wins.** Point them out, even if they seem small. Early wins build momentum and help everyone trust the process.
- **Expect hiccups.** Don't interpret them as signs the system is broken. They're just part of learning something new. Stay curious and adjust where needed.

Once the Pipeline is in place, you'll rarely need to overhaul it. It's a stable structure, yet flexible enough to evolve as your firm does. Over time, you might refine a stage or add more definition where it's needed. But most of the time, you're just working the system, not reinventing it.

Set-Up Focus

Now that we've covered the benefits of the Pipeline, I need to give you a heads-up—a warning, of sorts. I could've told you earlier, but you're more prepared to hear it now.

Ready?

Once your Pipeline is fully up and running, you're going to encounter something unexpected. It's been there, lurking quietly in the shadows, waiting to make its move.

What's that?

Free time.

Yes, you read that right. Actual honest-to-goodness, what-do-I-do-with-my-hands free time.

After years of chasing one crisis after another, you'll suddenly find yourself with hours, maybe even whole days, where your firm runs without you. And while that might sound like a dream, it might even feel a bit unsettling.

You're used to the constant motion—the pressure, the pace, the adrenaline. But when the Pipeline does its job, when your team owns their roles and your cases keep moving, your job shifts. You're no longer in the weeds; you're steering the business.

So, what will you do with that time?

Maybe you'll focus on growth: finally expand your practice, deepen relationships, or pursue those big-picture goals you've shelved. Or maybe, for the first time in a long time, you'll actually get to *live*. Leave at a reasonable hour. Take that vacation. Go off the grid. And all the while, your firm won't skip a beat.

It can feel strange when the dust settles. But that calm is the reward. That's the future you've been building toward.

So, consider this your heads-up. Once the Pipeline is in place, you'll have time. What you do with it is up to you.

And if you're ready to start mapping your own Pipeline but aren't sure where to begin, check out the Quick-Start Guide. It's not everything but it's enough to help you get going. When you're ready to go deeper, The Set-Up workbook will walk you the rest of the way.

But even the best system in the world can't run itself. A Pipeline is only as strong as the people who bring it to life. That's what we'll focus on next: your People. The *heart* of the work. The drivers of the system. The ones who turn that structure into something extraordinary.

people

our core

BACK IN 2012, Google set out to answer a deceptively simple question: What makes great teams great?

They called it Project Aristotle. With all their brainpower, you'd think they'd already have the answer. They assumed it must come down to raw talent, high IQs, or maybe just having an exceptional leader. I'd have thought so, too.

But what they found surprised everyone.

For two years, they studied 180 different teams, analyzing more than 250 attributes. They looked into how teams communicated. Did everyone get a chance to speak up, or did one person dominate? They examined work habits, decision-making processes, and how teams handled conflict. They even mapped out personality types and leadership styles, all in search of that one thing, that magical ingredient that makes the best teams stand out.

And after all that research and all that time, it turns out the thing that made the biggest difference, that accounted for the best teams, wasn't talent, or intelligence, or even a charismatic leader. It was something else entirely.

Psychological safety.

That's right. The best teams weren't the ones stacked with A+ players. They were the ones where people felt *safe*. Safe to speak up, ask questions, share ideas, and even make mistakes. No fear of judgment. No pressure to perform perfectly. Just an environment where everyone felt they belonged. Trust. Openness. Connection. That's what made the difference.

Psychological safety sounds simple. But in most law firms, it's rare. It requires leaders to give up control, admit when they're wrong, and listen more than they speak. And that flies in the face of what most of us have seen.

And we've all been told that competitive pay, decent benefits, and a few perks along the way are enough. That if we make an offer attractive enough, the best people will come and stay. That our teams will perform the way they're supposed to.

But apparently, it doesn't work that way.

Because it's not just about the offer or how much you're willing to pay. It's about the environment people walk into. Do they feel respected? Heard? Safe to ask questions or admit mistakes without worrying about blame?

Still, we keep falling into the same patterns.

We assume the problem is the person. So, when someone underperforms, we don't ask what might have contributed to it. We just replace them. Fire fast, right? It feels like good leadership, like we're protecting the culture.

Then we go looking for someone better. Stronger. That unicorn who'll finally get it right. But when that person struggles, too, we don't stop to question the culture they just walked into. We blame the market. "There are no good people out there," we say.

But the truth is, even good people can't succeed in the wrong environment.

And chasing unicorns won't fix that.

What works isn't perfection. It's creating a space where regular capable people can do exceptional work. That starts with psychological safety.

So, how do you create that?

It starts with leadership. And not the kind that relies on titles or authority, but the kind that earns trust, sets the tone, and fuels motivation. What's missing in most conversations about law firm success these days is exactly that—leadership. That's why this part begins with three chapters on it; it's just that important.

From there, we'll get into the deeper purpose behind your firm, because chasing big cases or bigger fees isn't enough to hold a team together. You need a purpose that grounds and galvanizes your people.

Then we'll talk about how to build a value-driven team, one that's aligned, committed, and moving in the same direction.

Because what separates good firms from great ones isn't perfect people. It's the culture they're working in. That's the foundation your People pillar depends on.

5

It All Depends on You

Not everything that is faced can be changed,
but nothing can be changed until it is faced.
JAMES BALDWIN, "As Much Truth as One Can Bear"

MAY I BE BLUNT?

I'm sorry, but this is *so* important, I feel I must be.

I'm sure you've heard it said that an organization is only as good as its people. But the fact is: *It is only as good as its leader.*

You might want to let that sink in.

You see, I've been at this for almost thirty years. I've seen a lot of law firms—the brilliant, the broken, and the downright disasters. And the major thing I've noticed is that teams plagued by dysfunction, disconnection, and burnout are not being effectively led. They simply aren't. They may have a "leader" or "leaders," but not ones truly invested in being a Phenomenal Leader for their teams, which is absolutely foundational to a firm's success and well-being.

It's a harsh reality, but it's true.

If your firm is suffering in any way, the first place to look is at *you*, the leader. Truly. Whether it's underperforming team members, broken systems, or inconsistent cash flow, follow the trail, and inevitably it leads back to you and your leadership.

Sure, your firm might be led by multiple partners, but that doesn't let anybody off the hook. In fact, it's just the opposite. When you have multiple leaders, if even one of you isn't fully committed or is out of sync, it can throw the whole thing off. One partner might be committed to trying something new, while another resists change. This creates a tug-of-war that stalls progress. And it's why *each* of you must own your role, not just in the firm's success, but in its struggles, too.

I know this can be uncomfortable to hear. It's a tough burden to bear on top of everything else you carry. And I know that some of you have put everything on the line when you started your firm—your reputation, your bank account, your personal time with family and friends, and maybe even your marriage. All those sacrifices. All that hard work. So, when things go wrong, it's natural to look outside of yourself to find the source of your issues.

Owning a law firm is exhausting, physically and emotionally. No one could blame you for thinking, "If only I had better team members," or "If only my competitors didn't have such huge budgets," or "If only we could get more clients in the door."

But we must face that these challenges, as real as they feel, are often just symptoms of deeper leadership issues. Your firm is a mirror of your leadership style. It reflects your strengths, your weaknesses, and the ripple effects of your actions. And if your leadership skills stink, you and your firm won't reach their full potential. Period.

John Maxwell, a business expert who's spent decades writing and speaking about leadership, has a term for this, "The Law of the Lid," meaning that an organization's ability to succeed is limited by its leader's ability to lead.

So, it all comes down to us. There's no other way to say it. That's just the rub of owning your own firm. And we must honor this responsibility. Embrace it. Treat it like it's our most important job—because it is. It's not being the best lawyer in your firm. It's not having all the answers. It's not how well you market. It's *leading*.

Yet most law firm owners don't ever stop to think about their leadership at all. We're too busy, caught in the craziness of everything

Improve your leadership,
and you unlock everything else.

else, to realize just how much the success of it all depends on how well we're leading.

Plus, we're lawyers. Aren't lawyers by their very nature "leaders"?

Yeah, not so much.

The truth is leadership isn't something we just naturally "get." And we can't push it aside and pull a Scarlett O'Hara in *Gone with the Wind*, thinking we'll deal with it tomorrow.

If we want our firms to soar, to truly leave a mark, we've got to look it in the eye—our fear, our resistance—and shape a new identity for ourselves, stretching beyond our comfort zones. That means growing. Constantly. *As leaders*.

And that growth has to be our top priority.

Because it isn't just about us. It's about unlocking the full, untapped potential of our firms and everyone in them. It means shaping and nurturing your firm's DNA so it's not just you, but your entire team, invested in the health and well-being of the firm.

Yes, Maxwell's Law of the Lid is a tough pill to swallow, no doubt, but it also shows us the way forward: Improve your leadership, and you unlock everything else.

And that brings us to something most firm owners don't even realize they're shaping—their firm's climate.

There Are No Soloists Here

I don't know if you've noticed, but I don't call my team "employees."

The word implies a hierarchy, as if they are somehow less important than I am. They're not. Each person plays a vital role in our firm's success, and no single person carries the day. Not even me.

Before law school, I spent four years teaching junior high vocal music. Leading a choir meant working with a group of singers with varied voices, experiences, and (oh the) attitudes. My job was to blend these into a harmonious sound.

But I couldn't just rely on one standout singer to carry the group; that would've ruined the balance. Instead, I had to teach them to sing together—to listen and to match each other's volume, tone, and pitch.

We must do the same with the people who honor (yes, honor) us by working at our firms. We must treat them as the diverse, talented group of human beings they are, each with unique experiences and roles. Every one of them matters.

When we see each individual as an integral part of a cohesive team—not just as someone there to get a job done—we create a firm where every person feels valued, motivated, and connected to something greater.

Your Firm's Climate

Now, I want to be clear here. I'm not talking about culture, a word that is often thrown around but just as often misunderstood. Culture is deep-rooted. It's the collective values and behaviors that evolve over time.

But *climate*? That's different. Culture is what your team believes; climate is what they *feel*. While culture is the bedrock of your firm, climate is the weather.

You may not have heard it put this way, but I bet you know exactly how it feels.

Climate is the day-to-day vibe in your firm, the experience of what's happening *right now*. It's that little catch in the air after a difficult conversation, or those sharp words that leave the team on edge. It's those fleeting stressful moments that don't pass unnoticed.

Unlike culture, which evolves over time, climate can shift in an instant, like a sudden rainstorm in the tropics. One great moment—like a big case settling or a team member getting publicly recognized—can lift the whole team. But just as quickly, a tense exchange or a sudden change in direction can deflate confidence and throw everything off.

A positive climate
is shaped every
single day—by you.

Climate is a silent player, constantly influencing how your team feels, performs, and collaborates. And it can be sneaky. You think things are just fine, and then one conversation, one decision, one sideways glance, and suddenly the air shifts. You can't quite put your finger on it, but you feel the shift. Something's off. People are quieter, emails sound passive-aggressive, and the energy of the team feels like it's been sucked out of the office.

Now, why am I putting such an emphasis on climate?

Because your firm's climate is a direct reflection of your leadership. It mirrors your decisions, your tone, and the example you set every day. And surprisingly, your firm's climate has a huge impact on your bottom line. In fact, almost a third—yes, one-third—of your financial results—your Profitability—comes down to your firm's climate.

Let's think of it like this.

Say your firm is an Indy car. Sleek, powerful, and built to win. But it doesn't matter how fast or precise it's designed to be if the driver's all over the place. With a steady, confident driver at the wheel, the car takes turns smoothly, handles surprises without breaking a sweat, and gets to the finish line in one glorious piece.

But if the driver is unsure, inconsistent, or second-guessing every move, the car struggles. It hesitates, misses opportunities, and stalls out before it ever hits its stride.

Similarly, when you're steady, clear, and focused, the climate reflects that. The firm's results reflect that. The team trusts you, collaborates naturally, and momentum builds without unnecessary drama.

But if your leadership feels more like stop-and-go traffic—jerking forward one moment, slamming on the brakes the next—it creates friction that slows everyone down and stalls any progress you were working toward.

That's why a steady climate isn't optional. It creates the conditions for your team to shine. When the climate is consistent, people feel supported enough to take risks, get creative, and do their best work. It's the foundation for trust, strong performance, and the kind of client confidence that sets your firm apart.

And it all starts with *you*, hands on the wheel, choosing how to steer.

The tricky part?

Most of the time, we don't even realize the impact we're having. Feedback trickles in—a passing comment here, a small complaint there. Someone grumbles about not feeling heard in a meeting. Someone else is frustrated because expectations weren't clear. Alone, they seem small. Together, they tell a story. And if you're not listening, they quietly chip away at your firm's foundation—morale, performance, and, yes, even profitability.

That's why it's so important to pause and take a good, honest look at your firm's climate. Not just in the big moments, but in the quiet ones, too. The sighs, the silences, the sarcasm. They're all telling you something you can't afford to ignore.

So how do you figure out what's real and what's just the noise in your head?

There are six specific climate elements you can watch for, clear indicators of how it feels to work under your leadership. Whether your team feels steady or scattered, connected or just getting through the day, these elements offer a window into the experience you're shaping.

In the table below, the climate elements are laid out with reflection questions and the insight each one offers. These are research-backed markers that reveal what's working, what's not, and where your leadership might need refinement.

Climate Element	Question to Consider	Insight/Impact
Flexibility	Can team members get things done without red tape or being second-guessed?	Trust your team to make decisions, and they feel empowered. Micromanage them, and they feel stifled.
Responsibility	How much ownership do team members feel toward the firm and its clients?	When they see their contributions matter, they're more invested. If they feel sidelined, they won't be.
Performance Standards	Are the standards and expectations clear and consistently upheld by you?	Consistency here sets the bar for what's acceptable and prevents confusion and frustration.
Feedback and Rewards	Is your feedback fair, specific, and aligned with actual contributions?	Constructive feedback builds trust and motivation. Vague or inconsistent feedback doesn't.
Clarity	Does your team clearly understand the firm's mission and values?	If your team doesn't know where you're headed, they can't help you get there.
Commitment	How dedicated is each team member to a common purpose?	If you don't show commitment, why should they?

Climate Check-In

Set-Up Focus

I know how easy it is to simply tune out your firm's climate—say, like the elevator Muzak version of "Smells Like Teen Spirit." It plays quietly in the background—no lyrics, no distortion—just a hollow loop where the soul used to be. The original was raw, a full-body shout. But this version's been neutered. Think rage in a beige sweater.

That's exactly what a firm's climate can become when you don't pay attention. Familiar on the surface but missing all the things that made it worth listening to in the first place.

But climate isn't background noise. It's your weather system. And like any system, it doesn't just show up. It's created.

Which means someone is setting the tone. And if you're the leader, that someone is you.

When you focus on the climate elements—flexibility, responsibility, performance standards, feedback and rewards, clarity, and commitment—you gain the power to shape the way your team feels, how they function, and how they show up for each other.

So, take a minute. Sit with this. How are you doing in these areas? Is your climate the kind that feels solid, steady, hopeful? Or are there pockets of unease, places where tension lingers or things still feel a bit wrong? That's worth paying attention to.

Because a positive climate doesn't just roll in like a cold front on a hot August day. It's shaped *every single day* in the big decisions, the small gestures, the tone you set when you're tired, when you're frustrated, or when you'd rather cancel the meeting and hide behind your door.

So, when things don't feel right in the firm, don't start with "What's wrong with my firm?"

Now you know better. Now you know the more honest question, the one that actually helps: "What kind of leader am I?"

In the next chapter, we'll dig into that. You'll meet six leadership archetypes—those familiar patterns of leading (or surviving) that you'll probably see in yourself, or at least in a boss who made you swear you'd never do things *that* way. But know this: Seeing yourself clearly is where it all starts.

6

What Kind of Leader Are You, Really?

There is nothing noble in being superior to your fellow man; true nobility is being superior to your former self.
W.L. SHELDON, *Ethical Addresses*

LET'S TAKE a stroll down memory lane. Think back to the first time you were in charge of a group of people.

Maybe you coached a baseball team, trying to keep a bunch of kids in the outfield from picking dandelions. Or you were student council president, organizing the prom or negotiating with the principal for better vending machine snacks. Maybe you were the smarty-pants who led law review, defending the Oxford comma while dragging everyone else to the finish line.

Whatever the case may be, how did you go about getting the results you were after? In other words, how did you lead? Are you still leading the same way today? And is it getting you the results you're after?

Really think about it. Self-awareness, after all, is the cornerstone of effective leadership.

I remember my first attempt at leadership.

It's the start of football season in 1981. I'm in ninth grade, smack dab in the middle of the cacophony that is the Kerr Junior High

School band room. My friend Vonda and I, freshly anointed drum majors, take on the monumental job of wrangling about a hundred rowdy eighth- and ninth-grade classmates to start the day by warming up with scales.

Each morning, amidst the uproar of voices, the clatter of instrument cases, and the sounds of trumpet players clearing the spittle from their horns and clarinet players testing their reeds, we dive headfirst into our roles. Armed with nothing but our lofty new title—"drum major"—and the naïve belief authority comes through sheer volume, we attempt to get things underway.

Mr. G., our lovely (and cigarette-loving) band director, disappears into his office to puff away, leaving us to navigate the pandemonium. We holler. We stomp. We blow our whistles like crossing guards on a power trip.

Suffice it to say, we didn't get much done—other than pissing everybody off.

Fast-forward thirty-plus years to when I started my firm. I had a vision for a firm where people had each other's backs. Where growth was shared and everyone was pulling in the same direction. I instinctively knew my early leadership style wouldn't cut it.

I mean, who wants to follow a leader who barks orders and leads with passive-aggressive sighs? I'm surely not raising my hand. Why would my team?

I needed a leadership reboot. A transformation.

So, I started researching leadership styles that resonated with who I was and what I wanted my firm to be. That work led to six leadership archetypes. Some are drawn from established leadership models; others shaped from what I saw, lived, or learned firsthand. They represent the patterns I kept coming back to, distilled from books, conversations, real-life missteps, and hard-earned clarity.

In the following pages, we'll walk through each of them. You'll likely spot pieces of yourself in all six. A few might hit a nerve. One or two might feel just right. But all of them will help you see yourself more clearly and grow closer to becoming what I call a Phenomenal Leader—someone who inspires and motivates their team to want success for the firm just as much as they do.

I'll warn you, though, this section covers a lot of ground, so you might want to grab a coffee or take a bio break first. Then come back ready to lean in, because understanding these archetypes is one of the fastest ways to improve how you lead.

Shaping Your Leadership Style

My journey toward Phenomenal Leadership started the same way I asked you to begin: by looking at my early leadership style and comparing it to the firm I envisioned. I needed to make a raw assessment of my natural tendency (my reptilian fallback, I'd say) and see how it fit with the team I wanted to build.

The idea was that if I could see what I instinctively did to lead before life experience began to shape me with (a little bit of) wisdom and restraint, I could understand how I might naturally react in times of crisis; in other words, I could discover what my default mode might be.

The same is true for you.

Your instinctive leadership style—the stuff you do without thinking—often comes from your most primal self. Think fight-or-flight mode. This comes directly from your ego, which is not particularly interested in doing what's right for other people. It's focused on keeping you safe, in control, or right.

In overwhelming moments, that instinct can take over, pulling you away from the vision you've worked so hard to build. Maybe you snap at a team member in frustration, creating so much fear and tension others are hesitant to speak up or share ideas. Or maybe you give up control entirely, avoiding tough calls and letting confusion settle in. Either way, you end up with a toxic environment where team members feel unsupported, and the firm's healthy climate begins to evaporate as engagement and motivation disappear.

Just recognizing these patterns in yourself is a major step forward. But that kind of recognition doesn't always feel good. It's humbling. Sometimes it stings. That's why, if you're going to do this honestly, you also have to do it with grace. Grace gives you room to face what's hard without turning away. It keeps you from shutting down or slipping into shame. It's what lets you take ownership without losing momentum.

With that kind of grounded honesty, you can step outside your ego and become more intentional about how you act. This way, even in tough times, you're leading with purpose and clarity.

And when you know your instinctive style and begin blending that awareness with proven leadership strategies, you put yourself in the best position to become the leader your firm actually needs.

The Authoritarian

So, what did I learn about my early leadership style—stomping around and barking orders? That I fit the archetype of the Authoritarian leader. The Authoritarian is the control freak who expects everything to be exactly as they say it should be. "My way or the highway" is their mantra.

The Authoritarian rules with an iron fist and an air of superiority, without an ounce of humility. Their leadership style feeds their ego with power and control, instilling fear and compliance in their team through intimidation, like a bully on the playground or me sharply blowing my whistle amidst the din of the Kerr Junior High School's band room.

I once worked with an attorney named Greg, the kind of tough-as-nails leader who definitely leaves a lasting impression. He was frustrated with a young lawyer for a poorly prepared brief. Rather than meet privately with the "offender" and explain the problems with the brief, Greg commanded everyone in the firm to go to the conference room for one of his infamous "firm meetings."

An uneasy tension hung in the room as everyone shuffled in, their glances darting to one another, waiting for the hammer to fall. No one understood why Greg had suddenly demanded their presence.

Then Greg stormed in, all in a rage. His face beet red, eyes narrowed, he waved the brief in the air. "Who the f*ck wrote this garbage?" he thundered. "We don't have time for sh*t like this. I've told you all a hundred times, if you can't handle the basics, get the f*ck out!"

Our roles are not simply to oversee our teams but to actively guide and support them.

The oxygen left the room. Shoulders hunched, eyes dropped to the floor, and the energy just drained away. Greg slammed the brief on the table, sending papers flying. I could see the young lawyer who'd written it staring down at his legal pad, terrified to make a move.

Geez.

You probably know someone like Greg. Maybe it's even you on your worst days.

This is the epitome of the Authoritarian. Sure, Greg's firm has won some big cases, and clients love his tough talk and promises to bulldoze the opposition. But behind the scenes, his team is falling apart. Creative ideas are crushed before they can take root because everyone's too scared to speak up or suggest a new approach. There's no trust, just resentment and disengagement.

Instead of inspiring his team, Greg's obsession with control has created an atmosphere of fear where potential goes untapped and loyalty runs thin. For every win in the courtroom, his firm loses a little more ground with his people. There's a quiet rebellion brewing that Greg is just too blind to see.

And that's the thing about this kind of leadership. It drains the life out of a firm's momentum. It takes us further from what we actually need: a team as committed to the firm's success as we are.

But there's still a lesson in this.

While the Authoritarian's approach is deeply flawed, their confidence and decisiveness can be powerful when used well. We learn from them the value of making swift decisions and standing firm in our vision. The key is balancing that strength with emotional intelligence—one of the most impactful things you can bring to your leadership and your firm's climate.

The EQ Edge

Emotional intelligence—your EQ—is the ability to manage your emotions while recognizing and responding to the emotions of others. It helps you connect more authentically, stay calm under pressure, and make smarter, more grounded decisions for your team.

It's also a powerful tool for client communication, tough conversations with opposing counsel, and persuading judges and juries. EQ helps you read the room and adapt in the moment.

And it's something you can strengthen. These five traits are skills you can build. With practice, they'll change how you lead.

- ***Self-Awareness:*** Get real with yourself. Notice your emotional patterns—what triggers you, how you react—and how those responses shape your decisions. The more aware you are, the more intentional you can be.
- ***Self-Regulation:*** It's not just about knowing your triggers. It's about managing them. Keeping your cool under pressure sets the tone for your team and builds emotional stability into your leadership.
- ***Motivation:*** Ask yourself what really fuels your work. If it's only about money or status, people will sense that. But when you're driven by a deeper purpose, like building a meaningful firm, your passion becomes contagious. And that sparks commitment in others.
- ***Empathy:*** Try to see things through your team's lens. Pay attention to what's said and what's left unsaid. Empathy builds trust, psychological safety, and better collaboration.
- ***Social Skills:*** Are you someone your team feels comfortable approaching? If not, start there. Strong leaders communicate clearly, address conflict constructively, and foster open, respectful dialogue.

The Absentee

On the flip side of the Authoritarian, there's a leader who turns over everything in the firm to someone else. And I don't mean they delegate things to an office manager, a paralegal, or another lawyer so they can keep their eye on the big picture.

I mean they just don't lead at all. They're never available to their team, never check in, and close their eyes to the reality of the firm and its health, thinking, "Hey, we're making money, what else matters?"

This makes me think of Jack. His firm is a revolving door of team members. You know the busy turnstiles at the Times Square–42nd Street subway stop in Manhattan? People go in. People go out. But they never stay. Yep, that's Jack's firm.

And Jack's a nice guy. He pays well. But people just don't stick it out.

Why? Because Jack is never there. He's either out playing golf with his cronies or at his lake house for weeks on end. His team usually has no idea where Jack is.

So, Jack's firm is led—if you can even call it that—by his office manager, Lisa. But all Lisa really does is make sure people get paychecks. Oh, and that they come in at 8:00 a.m. sharp, take exactly one hour for lunch—not a second more—and stay until 5:00 p.m. on the dot. Lisa, the drill sergeant.

The thing is, Jack's absence reveals more than just a leadership gap; it shows he's missing the subtle signs that something's off. His team is disengaged, going through the motions. Without his presence, Lisa (an obvious Authoritarian) has stepped in to fill the leadership vacuum.

By checking out, Jack doesn't just remove himself from the day-to-day; he sends a message that the firm isn't a priority. And without that anchor, the team is left feeling confused, directionless, and adrift. Where Authoritarian Greg holds people back by gripping too tightly, Jack is slowly eroding his firm through neglect.

And there's another type of Absentee leader we can't overlook—the one so busy lawyering they have no time for leading. This was me before I got serious about growing as a leader.

I have a colleague, Sarah, who's a powerhouse in the courtroom. But back at the office, she's more like a ghost. Her days are slammed with client meetings, depositions, and court appearances. Most of the time, she's buried in case files.

Sarah's committed, yes, but her team is left floundering, unsure what to do next. Questions go unanswered or get a quick, distracted reply. Team meetings, when they happen, are chaotic because Sarah barely has the bandwidth to prepare, let alone lead.

The vibe in her firm is like a rollercoaster. Morale spikes after a big verdict, then crashes again. The team feels undervalued, unsupported, and disillusioned. Take James, a bright young attorney who joined Sarah's firm, eager to grow. But after months of waiting for guidance that never came, he left to find a place where he could actually be mentored and seen.

Just like Jack's, Sarah's Absentee approach fails to unlock the full potential of her team and jeopardizes the health of her firm. For both Jack and Sarah, their lack of leadership undermines their firms' foundations, leading to instability and a revolving door of team members.

So, what can we learn from the Absentee leader?

The importance of being present and staying actively engaged with our teams. We need to be tuned in to the day-to-day operations and the overall health of our firms.

And I don't mean we can't delegate; we absolutely should. Nor do I mean we can't spend time on the golf course like Jack or focus on practicing law at the highest level like Sarah; if we stick to our Set-Up, we'll get there.

It's just, to be an effective leader, we must understand our roles are not simply to oversee our teams, but to actively guide and support them. We must recognize the invaluable necessity of consistent (note: I don't say "constant") oversight and being available to address issues as they come.

The Servant

Let's explore an archetype that might seem a bit unconventional in a law firm setting but has a lot to teach us about leadership: The Servant. In a profession where ego and hierarchy often reign, the Servant leader offers a refreshing, and surprisingly effective, alternative.

In the early 1970s, Robert K. Greenleaf introduced the idea of servant leadership, challenging traditional notions of top-down authority. His premise was radical: The best leaders serve first, putting the needs of others before their own pursuit of power.

Rather than leading from the front, with demands and control, the Servant leads from behind, with humility, support, and a deep commitment to helping others reach their full potential. I like to think of it as giving gentle nudges from behind, in a kind and, dare I say, *loving* way.

Not to get religious, but there's a scene in the Netflix series *The Chosen* that nails servant leadership. In it, Jesus sends his disciples out to teach and heal. They're nervous. "Heal the sick?" "Cast out demons?" They've only seen him do it. How can they possibly follow in his footsteps?

But he trusts them. He gives them authority. "Teach anything you've heard from me," he says. And when they ask what to do if they're rejected, he simply says, "Shake the dust off your feet."

That trust, that support, that gentle nudge forward—that's servant leadership. Instead of controlling from above, the Servant leader lifts their team, gives them the tools they need to be successful, and sends them out with confidence. And the result? In Jesus's case, a movement that changed the world.

Nelson Mandela said it beautifully: "A leader is like a shepherd. He stays behind the flock, letting the most nimble go out ahead, whereupon the others follow, not realizing that all along they are being directed from behind."

Servant leadership is about that kind of steady guidance: encouraging growth, building confidence, and empowering your team to shine. As John Maxwell puts it, "The heart of leadership is putting others ahead of yourself. It's doing what is best for the team."

Of course, no leadership style is without its challenges, and the Servant is no different. If you lean too far into service, decision-making slows down. Trying to meet everyone's needs all the time can lead to analysis paralysis, and suddenly, nothing gets done.

There's also a risk that team members might view the Servant as weak—a lap dog rather than a leader—which can undermine their authority. That's especially dangerous in our field, where strong, decisive leadership is expected and respected.

The key, then, is striking the right balance. Serve your team, yes, but don't disappear in their needs. Offer support and encouragement while holding clear expectations and maintaining kind, firm authority. That's what creates real trust. That's what allows your team to take ownership, grow, and thrive. And that's what builds a firm that can do the same.

The Coach

As I dug deeper into what it means to be a Servant leader, I realized the whole idea of being the boss felt outdated, like something that belonged in another era. The word carries too much weight, and none of it's the right kind. (Honestly, I still cringe when someone calls me "boss.")

I came to see that leading a thriving team takes a different kind of mindset, one rooted in service, but also a bit like being a coach. That insight got me curious about Nick Saban's leadership style and how he gets his teams to perform at such a high level.

Now, if you're not a college football aficionado, Coach Saban is undeniably one of the greatest American football coaches of all time. Not only was he one of the winningest, but he steered the University of Alabama's football team, the Crimson Tide, to *six* national championships. (My husband, a huge Louisiana State University fan, insists I mention that Saban also won a national championship with them. This is for you, Honey!)

Even if football's not your thing, Coach Saban has a lot to teach about leadership, especially when it comes to shaping your own style.

At first, Saban's leadership style looked a lot like what many of us have seen in traditional law firms: highly transactional and laser-focused on results. Everything came down to "What can I get out of this?" and tracking every detail.

"I was always a transactional leader. I was a very result-oriented person," Saban said during an interview at the 2024 HIMSS Global Health Conference & Exhibition. "Winning the game was most important. If we won, I patted people on the back. I was happy... But if we lost? I was very critical. It was always somebody's fault."

Your instinctive leadership style—the stuff you do without thinking—comes from your most primal self.

If you've ever worked under a transactional leader, you know how this feels. You're on edge all the time, tiptoeing through the eggshells to make sure you're not the one to blame when things go awry. Not to mention how you feel if you're this leader—the stress of always being on top is unforgiving.

Fortunately for Saban and every team he coached (as well as those fans!), he realized something had to change. This came to him as he prepared one of his teams to play a game he was sure they would lose.

It was during his time at Michigan State University. Before facing Ohio State's undefeated team, Saban, unsure how to prepare his struggling 4–5 team, called a psychiatrist. The advice? Keep your head down. Focus on one play at a time. Forget the scoreboard and just do your job.

And wouldn't you know it? That mindset change flipped a switch. They won. And from that moment on, Saban changed his entire leadership approach.

That shift captures the essence of what I call the Coach style. It's transformational leadership rooted in vision, discipline, and trust. Like the Servant leader, the Coach isn't driven by ego. They're focused on developing people and helping them become the best versions of themselves. Where the Servant leads through presence and support, the Coach leads through discipline and development, anchored by a clear vision and consistent, well-defined processes.

And the best Coaches strike a careful balance between long-term vision and short-term execution. Too much vision without follow-through leads to disengagement. Too much execution without purpose leads to burnout.

But when those elements work in harmony—when vision shapes the process and process supports the vision—that's when something powerful happens: The team stops working *for* a leader and starts working *with* one.

The Navigator

When it comes to leadership, some folks have a knack for seeing what's coming and steering their team through it with confidence.

The Navigator is that kind of leader—proactive, always thinking ahead, ready to guide their team through any situation. Unlike those who only react to problems as they pop up, the Navigator has a clear plan and keeps the team on track no matter what.

Think of it like Odysseus navigating his ship through the dangerous waters of the Aegean Sea.

If you don't remember it from high school literature class, in Homer's epic *The Odyssey*, Odysseus and his crew face a number of life-threatening challenges on their voyage home from the Trojan War. One of the most treacherous parts is navigating past the Sirens with their enchanting song, the six-headed monster Scylla, and the deadly whirlpool known as Charybdis.

Anticipating the dangers ahead, Odysseus formulates a strategic plan.

He orders his men to plug their ears with beeswax and has himself tied to the mast of the ship so he can hear the Sirens' song without being drawn to it. This allows Odysseus to steer his ship safely past the Sirens.

Then, facing Scylla and Charybdis, he decides to sail closer to Scylla, sacrificing a few men to the monster rather than risking the entire ship being swallowed by Charybdis. His foresight and decisive actions ensure the survival of most of his crew.

Like Odysseus, the Navigator anticipates challenges and formulates strategies to navigate through them. They lead with confidence, steering their team through both expected and unforeseen obstacles, ensuring their collective success and resilience.

As Jack Welch, former CEO of General Electric, put it, "A good leader remains focused... Controlling your direction is better than being controlled by it." Navigators get this. They know that waiting around for challenges to sort themselves out isn't an option. Whether it's changes in the law, new technology, or unexpected crises, Navigators roll up their sleeves, make the tough calls, and lead with grit and determination.

Yet, the Navigator must be careful. I think of the approach I took with the COVID-19 pandemic. In March of 2020, the governor of the

State of Oklahoma sent all but "essential services" home. Arguably, law firms fell into this category, but we decided to go ahead and send our people home. We have great case management software, which allowed us to keep working remotely.

But I hated not having everyone face-to-face. We're so much better together! So as soon as the state reopened, I called everyone back in. I thought I was being decisive and proactive. But I made a major mistake.

I didn't consider the real fear of many on my team about the spread of COVID and their concerns that our governor had acted too hastily (and perhaps politically) in opening things back up so soon. Not long after we reopened, we lost a team member who'd been with us from the start. I've always believed it was because of the way I handled COVID.

Listening to their concerns and addressing their fears would have been key to keeping up trust and morale. We could have come up with flexible options, like a gradual return to the office or continued remote work for those worried about their health. That kind of approach would have shown more empathy and understanding and struck a better balance between being proactive and thoughtful.

Here's the lesson: While a Navigator is who you want leading in a storm, they need to stay aware of how their actions affect the overall climate of the firm. It's about leveling the scales between being decisive and taking the time to hear out your team's concerns and perspectives. Sure, you need a clear plan to steer your firm, but you also need an open heart to make sure it's a journey everyone can take together.

The Magnetic Mirror

Let me introduce you to the last leader on our list—the one who's both a magnet and a mirror—the Magnetic Mirror. While the Servant supports and the Coach develops, the Magnetic Mirror reflects, helping others grow by modeling the values they want to see.

As a magnet, the Magnetic Mirror understands that like attracts like. They lead with integrity, transparency, and emotional intelligence, setting the standard for their team. As a mirror, they recognize that their team's actions reflect their own leadership, and they're vulnerable enough to look inward when things aren't going right.

This archetype is inspired by leadership guru John Maxwell, whose Law of the Lid I introduced earlier. Maxwell's philosophy is simple: Leadership is influence, nothing more, nothing less.

For the Magnetic Mirror, it's not about titles or positions. It's about influence and authenticity. It's about walking the talk, inspiring others by example, and guiding the team toward shared goals.

What sets Magnetic Mirrors apart is their commitment to creating leaders, not just sycophantic followers. They empower their team to grow, take ownership, and step up. And when you grow leaders inside your firm, *everyone* gets better. *Everyone* contributes to the firm's success.

For me, the idea of being a Magnetic Mirror especially hit home. When I decided to start my own firm, a close friend said, "You're doing this because you want to try cases and get a giant verdict."

And sure, maybe that seemed true, especially since I hadn't yet had the chance to first-chair a trial. But honestly, that wasn't it at all. What I truly wanted—and felt deeply—was to influence a change in how law firms operate and how the people inside them experience the work. Reading Maxwell's work made it clear: If I wanted to lead that kind of change, I had to shove my precious ego aside and lead with authenticity, vulnerability, and integrity.

Being a mom had already given me a sense of what that would take. Parenting is all about showing up, day in and day out, even when things aren't perfect. You have to model the values you want to see in your kids. If you want them to grow up to be independent, empathetic, and strong, you've got to be those things yourself.

Some days, I saw it come through. My kids would show kindness when it would've been easier not to. They'd take responsibility. They'd bounce back from something hard without crumbling. And I'd think, "Okay... we're getting there."

But there were other days when I didn't like what I saw reflected back. Days when I lost my temper or snapped under the pressure of juggling Delaney's unique challenges with autism while racing to keep up with Alex's relentless theater schedule. And sure enough, I'd hear my own tone echoed in theirs. I'd see my stress mirrored in their reactions. They learned from my rough days just as much as from my good ones.

That's what being a Magnetic Mirror is all about. It's not about being perfect. (Who's that?) It's about being real. It's about showing your team the values you want them to embody—and being honest when you fall short. Owning up, taking responsibility, and committing to doing better next time is what it's all about.

And just like with parenting, a Magnetic Mirror knows their role is to help their team members "grow up." You support them as they develop into leaders, letting them make their own decisions and take ownership of their roles—even if it means they stumble along the way. That's how you build a team that's strong, resilient, and ready to keep the firm moving forward when you're gone.

Of course, the Magnetic Mirror approach is not without its challenges. If you lean too heavily on personal influence, you might create a kind of dependency. Your team could start looking to you for every answer instead of thinking for themselves. And, honestly, who wants to be the helicopter parent of their team?

Then there's the emotional side of things. Always aiming for high emotional intelligence and constant self-improvement can take a toll. It's easy to burn out if you're not careful.

That's why it's important to build in some self-care and set boundaries. Make time for things that recharge you—whether it's meditation, exercise, or just a quiet walk. Decide when to unplug: no emails or calls after a certain hour. And take that vacation. Just a heads-up: Going to a convention or CLE out of state doesn't count.

At its core, the real power of the Magnetic Mirror is about inspiring and lifting people up. It's about integrity, authenticity, and emotional intelligence. When you reflect the values you want to see in your team and lead by example, you create an environment of trust and respect. And that's what gets people all in—not just for the firm's success, but for each other, too.

Set-Up Focus

Whew. That was a lot.

But then again, so is leadership.

Strangely, despite how crucial it is to our success, leadership can sometimes get dismissed as just a soft skill. Something a little extra. Optional. Like the kind of thing you circle back to after your "real work" is done. But that couldn't be more wrong.

Leadership *is* the real work. It's foundational. It's the infrastructure your People pillar is built on. It's what determines how your team functions and whether it holds together when things get hard.

That isn't soft. It's powerful. And that's why it can't be left to instinct. Or ego. Or whatever you absorbed from your worst boss.

The archetypes we just walked through aren't boxes to squeeze ourselves into. Nor are they fixed identities. They're patterns—of instinct, reaction, and habit—that show up in different ways. Some emerge when we're leading with confidence and clarity. Others surface when we're reacting from fear or falling into old habits.

You might have seen yourself clearly in one. Or found pieces of yourself in several. Or maybe none felt quite like you, but you recognized the damage (or inspiration) a style like that can create.

That's the point. Every archetype has something to teach us about what leadership can look like, what it costs when we get it wrong, and who we might become when we get it right.

But seeing it is only the first step. What comes next is how we change it. How we lead with more awareness, more consistency, and more skill.

That's where we're headed next: the tools to do it better.

7

The Practice of Phenomenal Leadership

The journey is the reward.
STEVE JOBS, "Quotations from Chairman Jobs"

NOT LONG AGO, while I was drafting this section, my husband asked me something:

"What separates a good leader from a truly phenomenal one?"

Hmm. Good question. It's the kind that cuts straight to the heart of what leadership is really about.

Is it confidence? Vision? The ability to motivate and inspire?

The truth is, it's never just one thing. It's a messier, more beautiful tangle than that—a patchwork of instincts, learned skills, personal values, and practiced behaviors. Some of these come naturally. Others, you have to work at. And some only show up under pressure, often in ways that surprise you. But when they come together with intention, that's where transformation happens.

It's like the '90s Bulls.

Do you remember? If not, bear with me here.

There's Jordan, with his man-on-a-mission scoring frenzy. Pippen, quietly brilliant in all the ways that don't make headlines. And (oh!) Dennis Rodman, just throwing himself into the chaos with that wild, relentless defense. Pulling it all together is Phil Jackson, zen-mastering the whole situation like some kind of wizard. Everyone's doing their unique and necessary part. But together, they were basically unbeatable.

Leadership works the same way. Only in this case, *you* are the whole team.

That's what makes leadership so demanding. It asks you to play every role: strategist and listener, visionary and grounding force. It means drawing on different parts of yourself: not just the instincts that come naturally, but the skills you've practiced, the traits you've sharpened, and the judgment you've worked so hard to earn.

Being a Phenomenal Leader isn't about doing what's easy or automatic. It's the willingness to know your full range, and the courage to lead from it every day.

What follows are the core practices of Phenomenal Leadership, each one drawn from the best, most effective parts of the archetypes we just explored.

Think of this as your next step from awareness to action, from reflective instinct to intentional behavior. If the archetypes help you see yourself clearly, these practices will help you show up differently. Together, they form the framework for something far more impactful than just good leadership. They form the heart of Phenomenal Leadership.

I hope you'll use them as a practical guide to revisit often as you grow your leadership style, strengthen your team dynamics, and keep becoming the leader your team needs. Because when your leadership improves—even by a few degrees—your firm improves with it.

Six Core Practices of Phenomenal Leadership

1. **Empowering Through Service and Support:** Leadership isn't about being the star of the show. It's about helping others shine. Great leaders uplift their team, provide the support they need, and empower them to lead in their own ways.

Phenomenal Leadership is never finished—
you earn it every day.

Bottom line: Serve your team by giving them the tools and opportunities to succeed.

2 **Staying Engaged Without Micromanaging:** The best leaders find the sweet spot between hovering over every detail and being completely out of touch. They know how to delegate, use processes, and trust their team to handle their responsibilities, while also staying involved enough to offer support and guidance when needed.

Bottom line: Stay connected but give your team the space to own their work.

3 **Balancing Confidence with Humility:** A great leader knows when to step up and make tough calls. You've got to be confident in your vision and willing to stand your ground when it matters. But unlike the Authoritarian, who rules with an iron fist, it's crucial to balance that confidence with humility—to listen, learn, and invite your team's input.

Bottom line: Be bold in your decisions but always be open to other viewpoints.

4 **Cultivating a Growth Mindset:** Think of yourself as both a coach and a role model. Invest in your team's growth and lead by example. This inspires a culture where everyone values learning, resilience, and continuous improvement.

Bottom line: Encourage a growth mindset by always learning yourself and setting the example for others.

5 **Guiding with a Clear Vision and Purpose:** Like a good Navigator, a Phenomenal Leader charts a clear course and makes sure everyone understands where the firm is headed. This creates a shared sense of purpose that keeps the team focused, disciplined, and energized.

Bottom line: Keep your team aligned and motivated with clear goals and a strong purpose.

6 **Using Emotional Intelligence as a Leadership Tool:** Phenomenal Leaders know that understanding and managing emotions—both their own and their team's—is critical. Emotional intelligence helps you navigate tough situations, build trust, and keep everyone motivated and cohesive.

Bottom line: Develop emotional intelligence to lead with empathy and keep your team connected.

When you practice this part consistently, even imperfectly, you're not only growing as a leader, but also shaping your firm's climate. You're setting the emotional tone, the expectations, and the trust level that determines how your team feels about showing up every day. And, as you already know, climate isn't just about the weather; it directly affects your team's performance and engagement, as well as your bottom line.

That's why Phenomenal Leadership can't hinge on one big moment. It's not a mountaintop you reach, arms raised in victory. It's a daily practice—a steady, intentional way of showing up for your team, your firm, and yourself. The Bulls didn't stop after one championship, did they? They kept practicing, kept refining, kept rising. Because that's what greatness takes.

When you lead with that same relentless commitment—the daily choice to practice, refine, and rise—your team leans in. The weight doesn't fall on you anymore. It's shared. And together, you build a firm people don't just work for, but one they *believe* in.

That's the kind of Phenomenal Leader people choose to follow.

Set-Up Focus

It's time to close our journey into Phenomenal Leadership and move on to talk about those teams of ours. But before we go, I feel I must share something with you.

Even after everything I've walked you through—climate, the archetypes, the practical skills—I still wouldn't call myself a Phenomenal Leader. Not in the way I define it in this book, anyway.

Because Phenomenal Leadership is something you're always working *toward*. It's a journey. And it's not really a title you give to yourself. It's something you *earn*, something your team reflects back onto you.

That said, I *can* say this: The leader I am today is virtually unrecognizable to the girl who once stood in front of that chaotic band room, blowing her whistle and hoping, "Maybe today, they'll listen." She's even a bit of a stranger to the woman who started her firm over a decade ago, thinking passion and grit would be enough for a wildly successful firm.

I've come a long way. I've done the work—the messy, unglamorous, often uncomfortable work. And, yes, I've also led from ego. From fear. I've gotten it wrong. Sometimes painfully so.

Yet somewhere along the way, I also learned to extend grace to myself and to others. Because leadership isn't clean or easy or always intuitive. It's chaotic, emotional, and relentlessly human. But grace makes space for growth. It allows us to lead with both strength and softness, discipline and forgiveness.

And eventually, my commitment to growth started to render its receipts. I watched our team become something extraordinary. They trust each other. They support one another. They're proud of the work they do and the lives they help change. Our firm is stronger. Our Pipeline and Process are tighter. Our Profitability is more predictable.

If I can come this far, I know you can, too.

You don't need perfect timing or perfect confidence. You don't need to feel "ready." Just start. Pick one leadership practice that stands out to you. Maybe one that made you fidget a little, or one you know deep down is holding your team back. Focus on it for the next week. Try making one small shift: in a conversation, in your tone, in allowing yourself to let go a little.

Then, reflect. What worked? What felt hard? What might you do differently next time?

Next week, pick another quality. Then build on it, refine it.

And if you want help figuring out where to start, grab the Leadership Self-Assessment in The Set-Up workbook. It'll help you see where you are right now—and where you can grow next.

Now, our teams.

8

What Is Your "Why"?

Your work is to find out what your work should be… and attend to it with all your heart.
***THE DHAMMAPADA*, v. 166**

HAVE YOU ever walked into a room and could just feel the tension clinging to the air, like it's almost palpable? It's like those days here in Oklahoma when the air gets heavy right before a tornado. The sky turns this eerie shade of green, and the air feels thick enough to cut with a knife. The stillness is unnerving. A storm is coming, and we all know it.

From the outside, it might look like things are great. Cases are being won and money's coming in. But inside? It's a slow-moving storm.

Edginess hangs in every meeting like static in the air. People hesitate before speaking up, and even direct conversations stay surface level. You see it in guarded looks exchanged in the hallway, the closed-off body language. The way people start choosing jaw-clenched silence over honesty. You might not be able to explain it, but you can feel it—that low hum of anxiety pulsing beneath the surface.

And that anxiety, that tension, doesn't just go away on its own. It's not like the tornado passes, and you're safe until the next one rolls through. Instead, it settles in.

It starts to shape how people work together—or don't. Slowly, but surely, left unchecked, that undercurrent seeps into the fabric of your firm, quietly undermining everything you've worked so hard to build.

And before you know it, it becomes your *culture*. A culture that lives deep in the DNA of your firm, like an invisible strand weaving through every aspect. A culture that subtly shapes how your team members think, how they act, and how they connect to one another and your clients. A culture comprised of the unspoken rules everyone seems to follow and the shared mindset that drives decisions.

Because culture doesn't wait for permission. It's always forming based on the climate you allow.

Default Culture

And there's the catch.

If you're not careful about it, an unwatched climate can quietly harden into what I call a "default culture." It's that underlying toxic vibe that forms when a firm's values and behaviors aren't being consciously shaped or guided.

Unlike the day-to-day shifts of climate we discussed in chapter 5, a default culture builds slowly and haphazardly, driven by whoever or whatever is most dominant. Maybe it's the loudest voices in the room. Or the unspoken rules about who's really in charge. Or just old habits that have gone unchecked for too long.

A default culture is what happens when no one is paying attention. It sneaks in slowly and quietly until one day you look up to realize the firm you dreamed of running doesn't feel like yours at all. And not because of bad people; not at all. But because talented, well-intentioned professionals get caught up in a mess of unspoken norms and sabotaging behaviors.

I know this all too well because I've been there. Let me take you back to a time in my career when I was part of a team operating under a default culture.

The firm I worked for was successful on the surface—lots of cases, high revenue, prestigious lawyers. But underneath, things were toxic. The culture we'd slipped into wasn't something anyone had consciously created. And it showed.

Every corner of the office held tension you couldn't miss.

The lawyers were all out for themselves, obsessed with who was getting paid more, who wasn't pulling their weight, and who the senior partners favored. You'd hear whispers about how one associate got a huge bonus while others got nothing, or how certain partners seemed to handpick their favorites for the plum assignments. FOMO—the fear of missing out—was rampant.

Paralegals would work only for the partner on the case, even if associates were drowning in work and desperately needed help. "I don't work for you" was the attitude, and no matter how small the task, it would never take priority if the right person didn't ask.

Support staff squabbled among themselves, amplifying their own importance, based on which partner they worked for. Loyalty wasn't to the team; it was to individuals.

Communication barely existed. The firm was notorious for closed-door "meetings"—just a select few lawyers huddled together, leaving everyone else to speculate about what was going on. The gossip mill would begin to churn at the sound of the door closing, as those left out tried to piece together the purpose of these secretive gatherings.

And trust? Let's just say it was a luxury none of us could afford. If you dared to share an idea or a concern, you could bet it would be twisted and used against you later. You simply never knew who you could trust.

This was the norm. Each person had their own territory and their own agenda. Everyone was so focused on financial gain or position in the ranks, the concept of working together as a team seemed foreign. We were just a collection of individuals, each trying to get ahead in our own way, without anything to unite us but the rat race of it all.

And I'll admit, I got caught up in it, too. Some of my colleagues may remember me as one of the favorites, but let me tell you, it was awful. There was just so much pressure and stress from the judgment and whispers, I'd gladly have taken a step back at any time.

A default culture is what happens when no one is paying attention.

But there's more to it.

The impact of a default culture can go way beyond making day-to-day life miserable. Over time, it chips away at the very foundation of your firm. Talented people won't stick around long. They'll either burn out from the stress or simply walk away, tired of trying to thrive in a place that hollows them out.

Clients will feel it, too, often before you do. It shows up in the little things: delayed updates, missed follow-throughs, short emails without warmth. But those things matter. They chip away at trust, and your reputation goes with it—because word gets around faster than you might think.

Eventually, the cracks get harder to hide. Innovation slows. The energy fades. What once felt sharp starts to feel sluggish. And the scariest part is you may not even see how far things have slipped until it's too late. What starts as low-grade dysfunction can turn into a full-on crisis that's hard to recover from.

The firm's potential sputters. And if nothing changes, your future flatlines.

The Missing Ingredient

But I have some good news. You're not stuck with the storm. Nor are you doomed to drift forever, trying to escape the death knell of a default culture. Even if the storm's already settled in and soaked everything through, there's still a way forward.

The missing ingredient? It's surprisingly straightforward.

You have to be clear, and you have to be intentional, about your firm's purpose. Your *why*.

And by that, I don't mean a mission statement collecting dust in a drawer or a list of values hanging in the lobby. I mean something *lived*. Something *real*. Something that shows up in every decision, every conversation, every piece of work your team touches. Something that shapes how your firm actually operates from the inside out.

Kind of like Patagonia's.

On Black Friday of 2011, while every other retailer was hyping flash sales and doorbusters, Patagonia took out a full-page ad in *The New York Times*. Front and center was one of their best-selling jackets. And just above it, a bold, unexpected headline: Don't Buy This Jacket.

Can you imagine? On the busiest shopping day of the year? But they meant every word of it—it aligned with their mission: "We're in business to save our home planet."

For most brands, it would've been risky; but for Patagonia, it was perfect. And when purpose is real like that, it's inspiring. And grounding. It gives people something to rally around, something bigger than profit or prestige.

And I think that type of clarity of conviction is why Simon Sinek's book *Start with Why* has hit home with so many.

His message is that the most resilient organizations aren't just built on *what* they do. They're built on *why* they do it. That purpose drives decisions, strengthens culture, and builds loyalty that lasts. It's why companies like Apple, with its culture of innovation, Harley-Davidson, with its cult-like loyalty, and, yes, even Patagonia don't just sell products—they create movements. Their why isn't a tagline showing up in ads. It's a throughline. A living force behind how they operate.

And that's a far cry from how most organizations—including law firms—actually operate.

Think about it. Most law firms are all about what Sinek calls the "what": practicing law. They talk up their services, highlight their areas of expertise, and boast about their track record. But without a clear why, it's all surface.

People start showing up hollow. They armor up and protect their territory, because when there's no shared meaning to hold onto, all you have left is what you can control. The work becomes transactional. Relationships become strategic. And slowly, everyone stops bringing their whole selves to the office.

But when you get this right—when you start leaning into your firm's purpose with your team—the impact is powerful. Just consider the research.

A meta-analysis of corporate purpose studies found that companies with a strong sense of purpose consistently outperform their peers. They report higher employee engagement, better customer satisfaction, and stronger financial results.

Gallup found that when employees feel connected to a firm's mission, they're more productive and more likely to see their work as meaningful.

And a study by LinkedIn and Imperative found that purpose-oriented employees are 54 percent more likely to stay at a company for more than five years—and 30 percent more likely to be high performers—than those just working for a paycheck.

We are wired for purpose. We need to matter. We need to belong to something bigger than our own paycheck or ego. When that's missing, we don't just end up with a default culture; we suffer. We become smaller versions of ourselves, as do our firms.

Simply put, having a clear why is not just the core ingredient—it's foundational. And it's how you move from default culture to intentional culture.

Game-changing.

Finding Our Why

And a game changer is what I was after when I started my firm.

Inspired by purpose-driven companies, I saw a chance to build something radically different from anywhere I'd worked before. I began by bringing in one brave soul, Harrison, who believed in that vision. From there, we started building a team.

And because we were starting from scratch, there were no rules, no legacy systems to fight against. Just possibility. We looked for people who were ready to challenge the status quo and reimagine what a law firm could be.

You see, none of us had ever seen a law firm embrace a mission and core values. (Not to say they didn't exist; we just hadn't seen any.) But we wanted to try it. We were convinced they were the key to ensuring we were fueled by the same passion—the same underlying why—that would counter the toxicity we'd all experienced in other law firm settings.

So, on a crisp February afternoon not long after we opened, our entire team—all our lawyers and each member of our support staff—gathered in a tiny conference room at the office of our business coach, Gene Hopper.

Gene, seasoned in business transformation, set the stage. We were going to brainstorm and define our collective why by crafting a mission statement and core values for the firm.

Armed with sticky notes and markers, each of us took some time to really think about what makes us tick—not just in the work we did, but why we chose to do it every day. What got us out of bed in the morning? What were the characteristics we wanted in our teammates? What was it about our work that felt truly meaningful?

It was hard for some of us at first. What's a value anyway? Gene explained that values are the guiding principles that shape our actions and decisions. They're the core beliefs that define what's important to us in our work and in how we interact with others.

For some, values may mean integrity—the commitment to always doing what's right, even when it's difficult. For others, it may be collaboration—the belief that working together as a team brings out the best in everyone. Values also include things like respect, accountability, self-motivation, and authenticity.

As we started jotting down thoughts, the room got quiet. You could hear marker caps popping on and off, the scratch of pens on sticky notes. One person wrote, "Do what you say you'll do." Another added, "Have each other's backs." Someone across the table said, "I just want to feel like what I do actually matters." Heads nodded.

We talked about clients who were hurting and how good it felt to truly help them. We shared what we valued most in a teammate: honesty, follow-through, kindness. It was simple and raw and unexpectedly deeper than any of us had ever experienced in a work setting. I remember thinking, "This is it. This is what I've been missing all these years."

As we talked, Gene began pointing out values most shared among us. These, she told us, weren't just individual values, they represented our collective spirit—our *core values*. She wrote them down.

Then, she turned our attention to creating our mission statement, explaining it should be a clear and concise expression of what our firm stands for and why we do what we do. A mission statement, she said, isn't just a slogan or tagline. It's meant to be the guiding principle that influences every decision we make and every action we take.

It wasn't long before we landed on something powerful: "To level the legal playing field for those mistreated by their insurance companies." It was an important moment for our firm. We'd all come together, leaned in, and agreed on something that defined us as more than just another law firm.

Fulmer Group Core Values

Client-Focused: We meet our clients in some of the hardest moments of their lives. We work with urgency, build real relationships, and aim to deliver results worth raving about.

Humble, but Hungry: We lead with curiosity and vulnerability. We ask, listen, question, learn, and then grow. We're always reaching beyond our comfort zone to do better.

The Power of Us: We know collaboration is our superpower. By bringing our full diverse talents together, we amplify potential and create something bigger than any one of us.

Do the Right Thing: Integrity is our nonnegotiable. We keep our promises, act with transparency, and do what's right. Even when no one's watching.

First Class All the Way: We strive for excellence in every detail. We want to be known by our clients, peers, and community as the best of the best.

Heart: We love what we do and why we do it. We let our passion fuel us.

Since that cold day in February, our firm has come a long way. Over the past eleven and a half years, four of the original eight team members are still with us. That says a lot about how strong our shared purpose is.

Yet as our team grew and new people came on board, we had to figure out how to make sure our values actually meant something. And we didn't always get it right at first. Each new hire (and the ones who didn't stick around) pushed us to either put up or shut up.

And as we grew, so did our *what*. We went from focusing solely on insurance bad faith cases to taking on personal injury and mass tort cases, too. The shift meant our mission needed to grow along with us.

Since 2019, our mission has been "Empowering Injured People." And it's not just about our clients. It's about everyone we encounter—each other, our community—because in one way or another, we've all been hurt. Our purpose is to help lift each other up however we can.

You might think that having a shared mission and core values would be enough to smooth the path ahead. We thought that, too. But we learned pretty quickly that wasn't enough. They're just words on a page, nice ideas that don't mean a darn thing unless they show up in our day-to-day. More on that in the next chapter.

Set-Up Focus

Mission statements and core values aren't new. But in the legal world, they might as well be.

I see these slick marketing slogans everywhere: "We Fight for You," "Experience You Can Count On," "Winning Is No Accident." We even had one in the beginning: "Not Your Granddad's Law Firm."

Yes, they're catchy... but what are they really *saying*?

Think about it. Can a tagline really carry a firm's soul? Can it ground you and keep you from drifting into the land of "just getting through the day"? The problem is real purpose runs much deeper than clever ad copy.

Defining your *why* isn't just a branding exercise.

It's a lifeline.

Because purpose and values—whether intentional or not—show up. They creep in through team dynamics, unspoken expectations, and the things no one quite wants to name. One day, you realize the loudest, grumpiest person in the room is setting the tone for everyone else. And somehow, no one ever voted them into that job.

That's why this work matters.

If you've never clearly named your mission and core values, now is the time. Not just "do good work" or "help our clients." That's a starting point, not a soul. Because naming your why is about grounding your People. It's a belonging thing.

There's an exercise in The Set-Up workbook to help you start this process. Please don't skip it. And don't do it alone. If you want your team to live the mission, invite them to help shape it.

Now, if you *do* already have a mission statement and values, great. You sat down, thought deeply, and tried to name what you want your firm to stand for. That's brave. But now comes the harder part: *Are those values still showing up*? Are they part of the conversation when decisions get made, or do they only come up during team retreats and website rewrites?

Because when values go silent, culture doesn't just freeze. It festers. Slowly. Quietly. Until one day, you have a toxic atmosphere no one wants to talk about. That's where an honest assessment becomes essential.

Culture Gut Check: Is Your Why Still Driving the Firm?

- When was the last time a major decision was explicitly guided by your mission or values?
- Do your team members ever reference them—out loud—in meetings or conversations?
- Have they faded into background noise, nice ideas that no one really touches?

If the answers make you squirm a little, that's okay. That's useful information. Culture doesn't collapse overnight. It fades. It drifts. But drift is something you can course-correct.

Start small. Pick one or two ways to reconnect with your why and build from there. The next chapter will walk you through how.

As the leader, your role in this process is huge. Changing a firm's culture is tough, I won't sugarcoat it. But it may be the most meaningful work you do. It just takes consistency. And honesty. And the courage to live the values you expect from others.

Because your culture is already forming, *with or without your direction*. So, shape it on purpose. Make it something people want to be a part of. Make it something *you* want to be a part of.

9

Putting Your Why Into Action

Don't say things. What you are stands over you the while, and thunders so that I cannot hear what you say to the contrary.
RALPH WALDO EMERSON, *Letters and Social Aims*

IN THE FRONT courtyard of my home, we have two matching flower beds—one on the east side, the other on the west. They're virtually identical: same size, same design, and same carefully chosen plants. In early spring, when everything's just been planted, I always think, "Ah, yes, this is going to be beautiful."

As summer kicks in, the bed on the east side is amazing. Basking in hours of sunlight, the flowers burst with vibrant colors, standing tall and proud. They reach their arms and pretty faces toward the sky, opening fully to the warmth above.

But the west bed tells a different, much sadder, story. It sits in the shade of a lovely large live oak tree I absolutely adore. Yet the tree steals the sun, and the flowers pay the price.

They struggle, their leaves pale. Their stems grow frail, and they languish. They try, I know they do, but I ache as I see them stretch toward the light they rarely find, knowing they'll never quite bloom the way they were meant to.

My courtyard reminds me a lot of our firm in the beginning. We had carefully crafted our mission and core values and felt proud. We were convinced we were planting something meaningful, something that could shape who we were and how we'd grow.

But just like those shaded flowers, our values started to wilt. We had them. We believed in them. But we weren't tending to them. Not really. Slowly, they started to fade.

And a challenge that would test us all was waiting just outside the door. Our first trial.

Embracing It

The trial—a bad faith case referred to us by another lawyer—was just weeks away, and the motions were piling up. Witnesses were unprepared, exhibits were scattered, and we were still scrambling to piece together our trial strategy. It was starting to sink in: We were nowhere near ready.

To make matters worse, this was my first trial as first chair. And, yes, I was excited about it, but with how unprepared we were, I felt exposed and unsteady. If we didn't pull it together soon, we wouldn't just lose the case and let our client down, but I'd feel as if I'd led the team into something I wasn't equipped to handle. That feeling is the *worst*.

And you could see this pressure's impact in the team itself. (You might recognize some of these folks... but as they say in *Dragnet*, "names have been changed to protect the innocent.")

Nancy—The Expert—stormed around like an air traffic controller trying to land a dozen planes at once. She barked orders left and right but hadn't handled her own tasks. Briefs sat unfinished and key witnesses hadn't been contacted. I'd prepped to meet with our client, only to learn Nancy had never scheduled the meeting. I shifted gears, trying to salvage what I could.

I made my way over to Jeff—The Hoarder.

His desk was a disaster zone—documents, Post-its, legal pads scattered everywhere. Jeff was buried somewhere underneath it all, typing like mad. He wouldn't let go of the brief, even with an hour to go before the deadline. "Just needs final touches," he muttered.

I pushed. He resisted. Delegation wasn't in his vocabulary. The runner had to turn around mid-route to the courthouse just to grab Jeff's last-minute masterpiece.

Part of Jeff's holdup was Tom—The Change Resister. Solid but stubborn, Tom flat-out refused to use our new case management software. None of the exhibits for the case had been uploaded. He had them somewhere, but nobody else could find anything.

Meanwhile, Emily—The Happy Camper—kept smiling through it all but defaulted to quick fixes instead of asking for help. She sent out our Final Exhibit List without first checking with Tom to make sure she had everything. She didn't. I had to scramble to get on the phone and beg opposing counsel to let us update the list.

It was chaos. Each member of our team had strengths. I mean, I didn't hire any of them by accident. But those strengths turned inward, colliding with the pressure of the trial instead of channeling toward each other. It was like herding cats in a tornado, each one spinning in a different direction.

And our values? The ones we'd carefully chosen and proudly posted?

Nowhere to be found.

Nancy talked a big game but didn't deliver. Jeff wouldn't let go. Tom refused to adapt. Emily avoided asking for help. And all of it, *all of it*, ran directly against the values we'd worked so hard to define.

But the real problem wasn't them.

It was me.

I was the one who let the values slide when things got busy. I hadn't insisted we live them in the day-to-day, even though I knew they would make a difference. I let them drift into the background.

Thankfully, the case settled. If it hadn't, I don't know what would've happened—for our client, for our fledgling reputation, or for the trust and morale of the team.

That experience slapped the idealism right out of me. I'd thought our values would hold up on their own just because we shared them. They didn't. Talking about values wasn't enough. We had to *live* them. Every day. In everything we did. *Without exception.*

Brené Brown puts this better than I ever could. In *Dare to Lead*, she introduces the idea of *living into* our values:

> A value is a way of being or believing that we hold most important.
>
> Living into our values means that we do more than profess our values, we practice them. We walk our talk—we are clear about what we believe and hold important, and we take care that our intentions, words, thoughts, and behaviors align with those beliefs.

Exactly.

When values are truly lived, you don't need to remind anyone what matters. You just feel it.

In the way people back each other up, pitch in without being asked, and speak up when something's off.

In the way the work starts to feel different, less like a job and more like a mission.

In how, when things get messy (because they always do), that shared commitment keeps the team going instead of falling apart.

But that kind of alignment doesn't just happen, no matter how nice you are or how many gold stars you hand out. Keeping values front and center takes work. Daily work.

And this is where a lot of law firms struggle.

It's not that they lack good intentions. I truly believe most firms do. But under pressure, when things get busy or stressful, values often quietly slip out of the decision-making process. And not on purpose. Just by neglect.

Slowly, the firm starts operating on autopilot. And that's when default culture can take hold. The values that once guided every decision begin to fade. The actions and behaviors that once reflected your principles start to drift. And before you know it, there's a growing gap between what the firm says it stands for and what actually happens day-to-day.

But it doesn't have to be that way.

Companies like Patagonia aren't immune to pressure. Of course, they face challenges. But they offer a glimpse of what it looks like to stay grounded in your values, even when the stakes are high. They help us imagine what's possible when values are more than just a branding exercise.

And I believe that's possible for you, too.

Because I've seen this firsthand. The last time we prepared for trial was nothing like that first chaotic experience. Same pressure. Different result. Why? Because we let our core values guide the way. We worked like a team; we were aligned. And it showed.

Living Your Why

So, how do you turn your firm's values into something more than a screen saver or pretty poster on the wall?

You embed them into the rhythm of the day—meetings, decisions, hiring, firing, all of it. The visible everyday actions that quietly say, "This is who we are around here."

What follows are some of the ways we've done that in our firm. Will they work exactly as written for yours? Maybe. Maybe not. Every team has its own quirks, personalities, and land mines. Take what fits. Tweak the rest.

And, yes, there will be skeptics on your team. Some folks may have been around long enough to have heard the core values talk before—at a previous job, or maybe even in your own firm—but never really saw it take root. Others may not quite see the point yet, not out of cynicism, but simply because they've never experienced what it looks like when values are actually lived. That's okay. Show, don't tell. Let your consistency do the talking. Give it time, because people begin to believe what they see repeated.

Just don't try to overhaul everything at once. Pick one or two changes that feel right. Start there and see what sticks.

Even small well-intentioned shifts—done with a little heart and a lot of consistency—start to rewire the firm's DNA. Slowly, almost invisibly at first, the culture starts to bend in the right direction. The noise quiets. The tension loosens. And that pretty poster on the wall begins to come to life—something your team can actually feel, rely on, and carry forward. Before long, it's not just a set of values. It's who you are.

Values don't live on paper—they live in what we do every day.

Decision-Making

Decisions are the heartbeat of any firm. They shape your day-to-day and define your long-term direction. But honestly, when you're the one in charge, decision fatigue is real. Everyone's looking at you with expectant eyes, hoping you'll make the right call.

So, how can you make sure you're getting it right?

The key is to let your values guide the way. Stephen Covey said it well: "Anything less than a conscious commitment to the important is an unconscious commitment to the unimportant."

It's not always easy. But one thing that helps is having a personal shorthand. It's a quick way to keep your values front and center, so every decision you make stays true to what matters most.

For us, that shorthand is a quirky little mantra: "Clients—Baby—Self." It's our way to let our values set the compass and keep our priorities clear.

(And, yes, calling the firm "Baby" might sound a little ridiculous—but it works. Just like raising a child, building a firm takes nurturing, patience, and continual growth. Even if you're not a parent, I'm sure you understand that it's a process. A loud, messy, occasionally beautiful process.)

Here's how our mantra plays out. Say we're deciding whether to take on some medical malpractice cases, a new field for us.

- **Clients:** First, we ask how this move would affect our current clients. Would it stretch our resources too thin to be client-focused? Would we lose our ability to meet them with heart in their hardest moments? Could it compromise the "first class all the way" quality our clients count on? If the answer is yes, we hit pause.
- **Baby:** Next, we look at the firm. Does this move align with our long-term integrity of doing the right thing? Are we being humble, but hungry—curious about what we don't know rather than overconfident? Do we have the power of us—the right collaborative team—to succeed in this specialty? If it aligns, we keep going.
- **Self:** Finally, we get honest about our motivations. Sure, med mal cases can be lucrative—but are we making this move because it

serves our mission or because the money looks good? "Do the right thing" means walking away if it's only about revenue.

Our mantra doesn't just make decision-making easier, it actually speeds it up. When we considered buying personal injury leads, the decision took minutes. The leads might've brought volume, but they would have disrupted the culture we've worked so hard to build. Our mantra gave us everything we needed to know. So, we gave it a quick "nope" and moved on.

If you want to make sure your decisions reflect your values, create a mantra that captures your top priorities. Use it as a mental checklist—whether you're hiring, expanding, or just trying to choose between two imperfect options (like deciding between a high-paying case with a difficult client or a meaningful case that barely covers costs). Stick with it, and you'll make better calls, faster. And your team will see it, too: Values aren't just something you say; they're something you live by.

Meetings

If you want your firm's values to actually show up in day-to-day behavior, start with your meetings. They're one of the few times when the whole team is in the same room. That makes them a practical starting point for reinforcing what matters and building habits around how you work together.

One way we bring our values into the room is with our daily 12 at 9:12 Huddle.

The idea of a quick daily team huddle isn't new. We borrowed it from business practices used by leaders like John D. Rockefeller and later popularized by strategist Verne Harnish. We've adapted the concept to fit our values and culture, and it's become one of the simplest, most reliable ways to stay connected and on mission.

Our huddle lasts just twelve minutes. It starts at exactly 9:12 a.m. And, yes, the weird time is on purpose. It catches attention and signals that this moment matters.

Everyone comes, ready to report on:

- **News:** What did we knock out yesterday? Just a quick overview of progress—wins, completions, forward motion.
- **Traffic:** What's slowing you down? This is the "call for help" section. We don't fix it here, but we schedule time to handle it. Unless it's a quick fix—then we knock it out on the spot.
- **Weather:** What's your focus for the day? Each person sets out their goals for the day so we all know where the energy's going.
- **MVP:** We give a shout-out to someone who lived our values in real, visible ways. It's quick, specific, and keeps us grounded in what matters.

That's it. Twelve minutes. Straight and to the point, with just enough structure to keep the team connected, moving forward, and focused on our shared priorities.

And huddles are just one way to embed values into your meetings. Here are a few others.

- **Value-Based Agendas:** Build time into your meetings to connect decisions back to your core values. Ask: "Does this reflect who we say we are?" If not, why not?
- **Values Check-Ins:** Start or end the meeting with a one-minute reflection: "Where did we live our values this week? Where did we miss the mark?" This doesn't have to be deep therapy, just honest.
- **Recognition That Means Something:** Don't wait for annual reviews. Recognize values in action right there in the room. You don't have to walk around passing out gold stars; just take a moment to name what you want more of.

Bottom line: If values aren't showing up in your meetings, they're probably not showing up anywhere else either.

Hiring and Recruiting

Struggling to find the right people? The problem might not be their skills—it just might be their values.

Too often, we hire to just plug a hole. Great resume? Law experience? Done. But the truth is, every hire is a *cultural* decision, not just a functional one. The right person raises the bar for everyone. The wrong one drags the whole team down, quietly killing momentum, morale, and trust.

I didn't always get this right.

I used to hire people who *seemed* like a great fit. Solid credentials, likeable enough. Sometimes it worked. But more often than not, it didn't.

Take Kent, for example. On paper, he was the perfect hire—great writer, knew the law. But when it came to how we work—like our Pipeline, our Process—he pushed back. *All the time.* And his resistance spread. Meetings got tense, and teamwork slowed to a crawl. Eventually, it came down to a choice: keep him or protect the culture we were building.

We chose our culture. (Not as quickly as we should've, but that's a story I'll tell you here in a bit.)

That experience changed how I think about hiring.

A resume is a snapshot. Skills can be taught. But values are baked into *who* someone is. They shape how someone thinks, solves problems, communicates, and makes decisions. You can't train someone into caring, collaborating, or owning their mistakes. They either live your values, or they don't.

So, we started hiring differently.

First, we put our mission and values front and center in the job post, making what we stand for clear from the beginning. If you're not interested in that, you're not going to enjoy working here, and we'd rather find that out early.

Then we ask every applicant to submit a cover letter explaining how their values align with ours. "Tell us how you've lived these values in a past experience." If they skip that step, they don't move forward, no matter how impressive their resume might be.

From there, the first round of interviews is handled by two people who know our culture inside and out—our litigation case manager and our director of marketing and client experience. If they're not convinced the person's a match, that's the end of the road. I don't even get involved.

And if we don't find the right fit, we don't settle. We just repost the ad and keep looking.

I know that sounds like more work and, in a way, it is. But it's made hiring easier, not harder. We don't waste time onboarding people who never belonged in the first place. We skip the drama and protect the team in the process.

So, if you're ready to hire differently, start here:

- Put your mission and values in every job post.
- Ask for alignment stories, not just resumes.
- Involve team members who live the culture.
- Don't compromise on cultural fit.

That's how you stop hiring for paper and start hiring for the long haul.

Terminations

I used to be terrible at letting team members go. I'd get that pit in my stomach every time I even thought about it. I'd push it off, thinking, "Maybe things will get better." They rarely did.

My problem? I was just too damn loyal. I'd watch poor performance drag on far longer than it should, like a slow leak you keep ignoring, not realizing how much damage it's doing until the floor's rotting beneath you.

Then, when I'd finally get the nerve to have the conversation, it was a mess. I'd show up with a laundry list of infractions, "Well, last week you did this..." or "Remember when you didn't follow through on that..." But it was never about just one thing by that point.

There's that old saying: "One bad apple can ruin the whole bunch." There's definitely a reason people say it. Remember Kent—the technically great hire who didn't quite fit? His constant negativity dragged everyone down. The whole team felt it, and I waited too long to act on what was best for our culture.

But I learned. Oh yes, I learned.

Ignoring problem team members doesn't make the problems go away. They seep into your team's daily existence and quietly impact everyone around them. Then the culture absorbs the dysfunction. And when that person finally leaves, the damage doesn't magically repair itself. You've still got work to do because culture doesn't bounce back on its own. You have to realign, rebuild, and earn back the trust that eroded while you sat there, too fearful to act.

Learning this, I knew I needed a better way to handle problem team members. Something that didn't let problems fester or let my misplaced loyalty stop me from making tough calls. I needed a way to catch things early and handle them in a way that felt right for me and the firm.

That's when I borrowed an idea from my husband, who was a supervisory special agent for the FBI. He used performance improvement plans (PIPs) to deal with his team in a firm and fair way, always clear about his expectations. We started using them, too, but with a twist. We anchor them in our values.

Here's how we handle it:

- **In-Person Meeting:** We never start with an email or a memo. These conversations are so important they start face-to-face, with laying out the goal to find a way forward that works for both the person and the firm.

- **Team Impact:** We connect the behavior to our values and how it's affecting the team. This helps shift the conversation from blame to alignment.

- **Specific Deficiencies:** We don't dance around the issues. We name what's not working and give clear real-world examples.

- **Revisit Coaching:** If we've addressed the issue before (and we usually have), we go back to those. This way we can confidently say, "This isn't new, it's a pattern. But we still believe change is possible."

- **The Plan:** Finally, we create a roadmap with goals, checkpoints, and timelines. The point of this isn't just for the team member to improve in their work performance, but to personally grow.

A PIP is designed to support improvement, but it also sets clear expectations. If things don't change by the end of the plan's timeline, the next step is termination—and that's made clear from the start. If the team member *does* improve, great. We acknowledge the progress, continue coaching as needed, and move forward with clearer alignment. It's not painless, but it's fair. And when handled this way, the process protects your culture instead of undermining it.

So, if you've been avoiding hard conversations or waiting for things to somehow improve on their own, try a value-based approach. Even if you've used PIPs before, center them around your core values. That's what turns a potentially difficult conversation into a chance to get honest and realign your culture in the process.

Performance Reviews

For the seventeen years I was at another law firm, we never once had a performance review. Not of me, any other lawyer, or any support staff. When I started my firm, I wanted to change this.

Feedback from our superiors is important. When we are left guessing how we are doing, wondering if we are missing the mark, we suffer unnecessarily. Taking the time to conduct performance reviews is a *kindness*. And it's key for providing clear feedback and recognizing achievements. Plus, it's a great way to keep your values front and center.

We approach them with a self-evaluation process, where each team member reflects on how well they're living up to the firm's core values. It's nothing fancy, just a page that helps our people pause and ask, "Am I actually living these values or just nodding along in meetings?"

It covers the heart of what matters most to us—things like being client-focused, staying humble, doing the right thing (even when nobody's watching), and bringing real heart to the work. Every team member rates themselves, jots down what's working and what's not, and reflects on where they could grow. I fill one out, too.

This practice not only reminds our team what truly matters to us as a firm but also gives us a chance to openly discuss our values and how we can live them out daily.

I'll never forget the first time a team member wrote, "I'm proud of my work, but I know I've been short with the team." It floored me—in the best possible way. That kind of honesty was a turning point, showing not only self-awareness but a real desire to grow. That's when I knew the self-evaluation process mattered.

On the flip side, it's a red flag when someone claims to be perfect in all areas. It signals a lack of reflection, and that runs counter to everything our core values are meant to build.

If you're not already doing performance reviews, I highly encourage you to start. When done right, they become a strategic way to support your People pillar. Schedule these reviews regularly, whether quarterly, biannually, or annually, to encourage ongoing alignment and accountability within your team.

Marketing

When I first started my firm, we mostly handled insurance bad faith cases. Most came through referrals from lawyers I'd worked with or had impressed over the years. So, I figured we didn't really need to do any marketing.

But we quickly hit a financial wall. Relying only on cases that take years to resolve just wasn't sustainable. We needed a steadier cash flow, and that meant expanding into personal injury work, which settles on a shorter timeline. Of course, stepping into the personal injury world meant diving headfirst into the maelstrom that is personal injury marketing.

You know how it is. Firms pour massive amounts into advertising on TV, radio, print, and billboards. The competition is everywhere! I still remember an ad from the '90s where these two lawyers were literally jumping out of helicopters. It felt larger than life, and honestly, pretty overwhelming to think how our firm—still finding its footing—could ever stand out without a huge marketing budget like that.

That's when we realized we didn't have to. We didn't need to be louder. We needed to be clearer about who we are and why we do what we do. I first heard Virginia lawyer Ben Glass talk about this value-based approach at a conference in Chicago, and it changed everything for us.

Culture doesn't bounce back on its own.

Instead of trying to outspend everyone else, we built our message around what made us different: our unique approach, our expertise, and our genuine commitment to knowing and understanding our clients. We focused on attracting people who actually *wanted* that kind of law firm.

We leaned into digital marketing: SEO, social media, thoughtful content. No helicopters, just a consistent message that reflected who we are and how we show up. Plus, it didn't break the bank.

And it worked.

We attract clients who aren't just looking for a PI lawyer—they are looking for *us*. They resonate with our values, trust our process, and make us better by being aligned from day one.

You can do this, too. Just focus on your values:

- **Tell stories that reflect your values.** Share real stories about how your firm has helped clients or contributed to the community in ways that align with your mission. Highlight the human side of your practice—the part that shows you care.
- **Create value-based content.** Write blog posts, make videos, or host podcasts on topics that matter to your audience and tie back to your core values. Show up as a trusted resource, not just a law firm.
- **Highlight community involvement.** Showcase your firm's engagement in local events, pro bono work, or charitable activities. Build real connections with potential clients by demonstrating your commitment.
- **Use testimonials that speak to values.** Choose client testimonials that highlight how your firm's values show up in action—whether it's about client care, transparency, or strong advocacy.
- **Showcase your team's passion.** Let your team share why they love working at your firm and what your values mean to them. Personalizing your brand builds trust, while showing the people behind the work.
- **Align social media with values.** Make sure your social media consistently reflects your mission and values. Share stories, insights, and tips that reinforce what your firm stands for.

Marketing doesn't have to be loud to be powerful. When it's rooted in who you are, it resonates. And when it resonates, it works.

Community Service

Living your values isn't just about what happens within the walls of your firm—it's about how those values ripple outward, touching the world around you.

When your firm actively engages with the community, it brings your mission to life in a way that words alone can't. Your community may know you as a law firm, but practicing law is only part of the picture. We have the chance to show them that we are so much more by engaging with them not just as lawyers, but as human beings who care.

Many of us already do this through volunteering, teaching, or serving on nonprofit boards. But there's something uniquely powerful about doing it as a team. Whether it's packing food for kids or supporting a cause you all care about, those shared experiences help your team bond, ground them in your mission, and remind them why they do the work they do.

So, how can your firm bring its values to life outside the office? Here are a few ways to get started:

- **Volunteer as a team.** Organize regular volunteer days supporting local nonprofits—food banks, shelters, community centers. This builds team cohesion *and* community impact.
- **Offer pro bono services.** Use your expertise to serve people who need it most. Pro bono work is a powerful way to walk your talk.
- **Sponsor or host community events.** Whether it's a charity run, a legal clinic, or a Know Your Rights session, give back where it matters.
- **Partner with local schools and colleges.** Speak to students about legal careers, civic engagement, or key issues in your practice area. Be a mentor, not just a lawyer.
- **Support local initiatives.** From youth programs to environmental cleanups, back the causes that reflect your values.

- **Create a charitable giving program.** Let your team help choose causes to support with a portion of earnings or hours. Give people a stake in giving back.

Set-Up Focus

Remember those two flower beds in my courtyard?

I spent a lot of time (and more money than I'd like to admit) trying to make them match. I planted the same flowers, used the same soil and fertilizer, watered them the same way. *For years*. But nothing changed. Graciously, a gardener friend of mine pointed out I was asking them to grow under the same rules in completely different conditions—and that just wasn't going to work.

With that piece of loving advice, I stopped trying to make them match and started trying to help them flourish. I chose plants that belonged in their space. Ones that could bloom where they were planted. And sure enough, once I did, something beautiful happened: The whole courtyard came to life.

Building a value-driven team is no different.

You figure out what actually works in *your* firm, with *your* people, in *this* season. It takes trial and error. And compost (literal or otherwise). But when you stop assuming things will grow on their own and start intentionally shaping the conditions for them to thrive, that's when your culture begins to truly take root.

And the real test is when things go sideways. Because they will. A storm will come through, a partner will leave, or a case will implode. And when that happens, your values are the thing that keeps you from getting swept away. They bring you back to center. They remind you of who you are and why you started this whole thing in the first place.

That's the promise of living into your values. When your team is aligned with shared values, everything else gets easier. Your Pipeline flows smoother. Your Process sharpens. Your Product gets stronger. And Profitability naturally follows.

So, think about the tactics we covered. You don't have to do them all, but you do have to do what matters and do it consistently. That's how real change takes root.

This work is never done. But when your roots are deep, you can weather anything. And you might just bloom brighter than you ever thought possible.

process

our engine

IF I EVER GET a next life, I already know what I'm doing with it: I'm going to be an interior designer. I'm a fanatic. I can spot a Saarinen table or a Bertoia wire chair at a glance, and I can always tell if it's a fake. But nothing compares to the Eames lounge chair. It's the gold standard of form meeting function. I have one in my office. It was a nonnegotiable when we designed our space.

We're in a building with a restaurant next door, and people are constantly walking past our office. Because of the glass front, they can see right in, and what they see first is the Eames chair, sitting there like it owns the place. People always assume we're a design firm. Honestly, that's a compliment, because great design just *does* something. It creates calm. It holds your attention. It makes a space feel intentional, like someone cared enough to think through how it would all work together.

Charles Eames, the designer behind that chair, once said, "The details are not the details. They make the design." And it's true. Great interior design isn't just pretty. And it's not just about the most expensive materials or following the latest trends. It's about design that works just as beautifully as it looks. The lighting is right where you need it. The cabinet opens the right way. The room invites you in and tells you exactly where to go without a single sign on the wall.

You don't always notice great design when it's working. But you definitely notice when it's not. It's like Barbie's Dreamhouse: no stairs, no doors, no plumbing. Beautiful? Sure. Livable? Not so much.

That's what great process does for a business.

Process is about the details—the small things that make the whole experience feel seamless. The thoughtful, unbroken pieces that work quietly behind the scenes, invisible when done right. It's what ensures your team works consistently, according to your high standards, and with confidence—no matter who's doing the work.

In this part, we're going to spend a little time on Process. And seriously—just a little—because this part is just one chapter long. But don't think it's because Process is an afterthought or the least important part of The Set-Up. No, it's one of the most important.

It's also the piece most law firms skip. And when they do, even the simplest tasks turn into time wasters. People reinvent the wheel daily. Everyone has their own way of doing things, which means nothing runs the same way twice and nothing is scalable. What's worse, you end up checking and rechecking work that should've been done right the first time.

With Process, excellence isn't optional. Consistency isn't accidental. *It's by design.*

If you want peace among your People, you need Process. If you want your Pipeline to perform, you need Process. If you ever want to step away from the day-to-day lawyering (or get back to it), you need Process to support your Product. And because every pillar feeds into Profitability, the role Process plays can't be underestimated.

It's the engine. The operating system. The thing that makes sure the work works. It's what keeps standards high and results predictable, no matter who's sitting in the chair. Just like great design, great Process disappears into the background. Because it works so well, no one has to think about it.

That's why Process is a pillar. It's what makes everything else in The Set-Up actually *move.*

10

The Invisible Engine

The most difficult thing is the decision to act, the rest is merely tenacity.
AMELIA EARHART, *Last Flight*

I'LL ADMIT, Process isn't sexy. It's just not. Outside of Andrea and Lauren in my firm, I don't know anyone who finds creating processes anything but tedious.

For the rest of us, it might just take a different lens to really see why it matters so much. So, let's get a little weird. Not full-on *Twilight Zone* or *Black Mirror* weird, but... close.

You know how their episodes always feel just a bit off? Like the world looks normal on the surface, but something underneath isn't quite right? And by the end, you realize there *is* a logic, just not the one you were expecting.

Kind of like this:

RICHARD'S WORLD: A Metaphor

EXT. CITY STREET - MORNING

The city hums with activity. Cars idle at intersections. People rush along the sidewalks. Storefronts open for business. Everything seems like any other morning.

RICHARD steps into the morning light, beginning his daily walk to the office. As he walks, small things catch his attention.

RICHARD'S POV

Cars sit idling at green lights, unmoving. People pause mid-stride, looking around as if unsure where they're going. Storefronts are open, but inside, there's no activity.

RICHARD
(*frowning, whispers*)
Huh?

He passes a BAKER outside a bakery, holding flour, eggs, and water. The Baker stares at the ingredients, confused, eyes shifting to passersby as though seeking answers.

Further down, CONSTRUCTION WORKERS stand by piles of bricks and tools, looking over the materials. But no bricks are laid. No walls rise. The building remains a skeleton.

Richard continues on.

He passes a TAILOR in her shop window. Fabric drapes over a mannequin, and her fingers hover above it, needle poised. She gazes at the cloth yet makes no stitch. The whirring of sewing machines fills the air, but no garments take shape.

RICHARD stops, scanning the world around him, a look of bewilderment on his face.

RICHARD
What's going on?

VOICE
Process.

The word lingers in the air like an echo. Richard shivers, unsettled. He scans the street: the cars, the baker, the workers, the tailor, all in motion, but nothing is moving forward.

Nothing works, because no one knows how.

END SCENE

Okay, okay... I know. A *Twilight Zone*-inspired script in a book about running a law firm is a bit silly. But sometimes a little silliness is the only way to tell the truth about what we might rather avoid.

Because if you've ever asked, "Did someone handle that?" or "Why does this only work when [fill in the blank]'s here?," you already know what it's like to live in *Richard's World*.

It's where everything starts, but nothing finishes. Tasks get halfway done. Deadlines get met, but just barely. You've got a strong team, but for some reason, they just don't hit the mark.

Sure, people may know what needs to get done. But they don't always know how to do it. So, they improvise. They build workarounds. They invent their own systems—some creative, some helpful, and some flat-out wrong. And suddenly, you're answering the same questions on loop. Like you're stuck in a different scene altogether. *Groundhog Day*.

And it *can* work. For a while. Especially if you've got strong people holding it all together. But that kind of system only lasts as long as the people in it. When someone burns out or walks out the door, things start to get rough. What once felt manageable starts jamming without warning.

Then instinct kicks in. You scramble. You patch things together. You cross your fingers and hope someone—anyone—really knows how things are supposed to go. The work might still get done, but it's slower. Sloppier. And the cracks begin to spider across every other pillar of your Set-Up.

Death by a thousand paper cuts.

In *Richard's World*, the people he encounters know what they are supposed to do—bake bread, build a building, sew a garment. They have the tools. They have the materials. But they don't have the method to bring it all together.

And that's the lesson of *Richard's World*: Good people and good tools aren't enough.

We need the invisible thread that ties everything together.

Process.

What Is Process, *Really*?

There's something we need to get straight about Process.

Yes, it's how you want the work to get done—step by step. That part's easy enough.

But in The Set-Up, Process means something more specific. It's not just a list of tasks. It's a *system* for how the work actually moves forward with logic, flow, and clear decision points built in.

I know that some folks hear the word "process" and picture a rigid checklist you follow blindly. But good Process is the opposite. It's flexible by design. It bakes the thinking into the doing, so your team doesn't get stuck or constantly come to you for answers.

In other words, it's not "Do A, then B, then C." It's "If this happens, do that. If it doesn't, go this way instead."

Good people and good tools aren't enough.

We need Process.

This kind of thinking first clicked for me in 1983. I was sitting in a classroom full of Radio Shack TRS-80s—early personal computers with glowing green text and a whole lot of personality. We were learning BASIC, one of the original programming languages. Our teacher, Mr. Melton, introduced us to simple logic: If X, then Y.

That was my first experience with algorithmic thinking—writing instructions that would solve a problem automatically. You didn't have to hover over the computer or intervene in its workings. You just had to build the logic well enough so the computer could run on its own.

That's what Process is. It's the algorithm that runs your firm.

Take something simple, like discovery responses coming in late. Your Pipeline Objective might be "Follow up." That tells you what needs to happen. And with your Roles, you know who's supposed to do it. But Process takes it further. It builds in the logic: "If the due date has passed, send a deficiency letter. Here's what the letter should say. If there's still no response in ten days, escalate." There's no need for anyone to pause or ask about it. The next step is already built in.

That's what makes Process so powerful. You're not explaining, correcting, or rescuing. You're just watching the system do what it was designed to do. It stabilizes the work. And when done well, it scales it. You stop relying on memory or the brilliance of one superstar. Instead, you rely on Process.

And remember: Process and Pipeline are two very different things.

> Pipeline provides the *direction*.
>
> Process creates the *movement* that enables the firm to run automatically.

When we first built the Pipeline, I didn't quite get this. I thought we were finished once the structure was in place. But over time, I realized something was missing. Cases were flowing, yes, but only when the right people had the right instincts. When someone was out or a new hire stepped in, progress slowed down.

We learned we had to treat Process as a separate pillar from Pipeline so we could give it the attention it needed. It's not a checklist, not a tool, but a foundational mindset.

Imagine one of those high-end, fully automated coffee machines—the kind that grinds the beans, heats the water to the perfect temperature, brews the coffee, and pours it into your mug—all without you lifting a finger. Once it's programmed, all you need to do is press a button or set a timer, and it handles everything from start to finish, delivering a perfect cup every time.

That's what we're doing with Process. It's like setting up a high-end coffee machine for your workflow. You give the machine—in this case, your team—the right input, like a clear Pipeline Objective, and they handle the rest according to your Process. As Michael Gerber put it in *The E-Myth Revisited*, "The system runs the business. The people run the system."

Why Me? Why Now? (Again.)

"But wait a second, Simone. Did you say it has to be me??"

I said it when we talked about Pipeline, but it's important to say it again. Yes, it *still* has to be you. But this time, the job is different. Back then, you were laying the groundwork: defining what the work is, who does it, and when it happens. Now? You're giving that foundation traction. You're turning vision into motion.

And just to be clear, you *don't* have to do this alone. In fact, you shouldn't. Bring your team in. Some of your best processes are probably already living in someone's head. Your job isn't to invent every step. It's to make what's working visible, repeatable, and shared.

"Okay, but we barely have time to do the work, much less write down how to do it."

That's fair.

Just yesterday, I spoke with a law firm owner who's handling cases, fielding questions, jumping from one thing to the next—wearing every hat in the firm. When I suggested she block off an hour or two to document a process, she hesitated. "That sounds great in theory, but when would I ever have the time?"

So, I invited her to try a quick experiment.

Think about how many times a day you hear "What do I do now?" Or how often you pause your own work to answer a question you've already answered before. Did you know it takes over twenty-three minutes—twenty-three minutes and fifteen seconds, to be exact—to regain focus after even a small interruption?

That adds up. Quickly. And it is expensive.

So, I asked her, "What would it be worth to get some of that time back?"

I pose that same question to you.

What if you carved out just an hour or so to document one or two core processes—onboarding, medical bill gathering, client follow-up? Honestly, it might not even take that long. Still, how many future interruptions could you prevent? How much focus could you reclaim?

You don't have to do it all at once. You're not building a machine in a day; you're setting the first gears in motion. Pick one area. Get that process running. Then track it with whatever tools your team already uses—a notebook, a shared Google doc, even a whiteboard. The key is visibility and follow-through.

When questions still come up, it's not that your Process is necessarily failing. It's feedback. If your Process needs a tweak, great. If it's clear and your team's just not following it? Smile and say, "There's a process for that." (Seriously. Put it on a sticky note. Make it your new catchphrase.)

And don't assume your case management system knows what you know. It doesn't. It only holds data, not judgment. It can track deadlines, but it can't capture the reasoning behind your decisions, the nuance of your strategy, or the context your team needs to move forward.

And the good news? You've already started. Your Pipeline is in place. Now, let's build the engine to drive it.

Building the Engine

So, where do you start?

You start by writing down the processes you're already using to accomplish your Pipeline Objectives. Don't overthink it. Just capture what's actually happening. Pick one Pipeline Objective and walk through it with your team or on your own. Start with the basics:

- What's the first thing we do when this Objective comes up?
- What happens next?
- Who's involved, and in what order?
- How do we know when it's complete?

Then dig a little deeper:

- Are there any decisions along the way?

  (If the client hasn't responded, then what? If the court date changes, then what?)

- Are there any approvals, exceptions, or alternative paths?

  (If we don't receive documents in time, who follows up? What's the backup plan?)

- Are there any conditions that change what happens next?

  (If it's a minor client, do we notify someone different? If it's out of county, does filing happen differently?)

Write the steps in order, including any if/then branches. You don't need perfect language or formatting. Just get the logic out of your head and onto the page.

Then review it with your team. They'll help fill in the gaps and point out what happens in real life. This is your chance to turn instincts and memory into something repeatable and reliable. One Process at a time, one Objective at a time, one Stage at a time.

Process Snapshot

- Start with one Pipeline Objective
- Write down current steps
- Add decision points ("If X, then Y")
- Review with team
- Document where it lives
- Test, tweak, train

As you work through linking Pipeline Objectives to processes, you'll likely come across some Objectives that don't have a clear process yet or have inconsistent steps. That's not a problem. Those gaps are actually opportunities to build new processes from scratch. We'll get to how to do that when we talk about artificial intelligence (AI) here in a bit.

Also keep in mind, if you notice multiple Objectives that follow the same general steps, don't overcomplicate things by creating separate processes for each one. Look for ways to streamline.

Let's say you typically send discovery and a protective order together. Turn that into one unified process. Or if your team always reviews discovery responses before scheduling depositions, make that a single, connected workflow. When you bundle related Objectives like this, you cut down on back-and-forth between team members and avoid overlapping steps.

I go into more detail in The Set-Up workbook, but for now, just focus on capturing what's already working well. You're not trying to reinvent the wheel. You're simply making sure it turns smoothly.

Where Process Goes Sideways

A great Process saves you time, money, and sanity if you build it to last. But watch out for these mistakes:

Trying to build for every exception: If you try to cover every outlier, you'll end up with a bloated Process. Focus on the typical case. Then give your team a solid foundation for handling the rest.

Over-documenting everything: Don't write a 30-page manual no one wants to read. Focus on the key steps, decision points, and handoffs. A good Process is clear, focused, and usable—not exhaustive.

Trying to launch everything at once: Rolling out too many processes at the same time leads to confusion. Start small. Get one working. Build momentum from there.

Skipping training and onboarding: If no one's been shown how to use the Process, they won't. Make time to teach it, revisit it, and explain the "why" behind it.

Assuming it'll run without reinforcement: Process isn't "set it and forget it." Without regular check-ins and buy-ins, people default to old habits. Keep it visible—for onboarding, team meetings, and daily use.

Letting usage vary from person to person: Process works when it's used the same way across the team.

Ignoring signs it needs a tweak: Questions, delays, or workarounds usually mean something's unclear. Don't scrap the Process, adjust it. Treat confusion as feedback.

Process Meets AI

Do you remember where you were when the news broke about ChatGPT? I do.

It was November 2022. I was getting ready for work, Coke Zero in hand, half-listening to the morning news. The talking heads were buzzing about this new AI platform that could write essays, code software, summarize documents, brainstorm ideas, and even draft emails. All you had to do was go online and start typing. *Wild.*

Immediately, I thought of the movie *Her*—the one where Joaquin Phoenix falls in love with an AI. Back in 2013, that felt like science fiction. Now? Conversations with machines are practically normal.

And the pace hasn't slowed. The tools keep improving. The use cases keep expanding. According to McKinsey, hundreds of millions of workers may need to shift careers over the next decade due to automation and AI. And if trends continue, it's not hard to imagine a future where the standard workweek looks very different than it does today. A two-day workweek might sound impossible now, but I wouldn't bet against it.

Process isn't a checklist.

It's a foundational mindset.

That said, I'm not sharing this to scare you. I really mean it as a wake-up call.

Because I know firms that haven't even implemented a case management system. They're still tracking deadlines on paper calendars, juggling documents across desktops, and relying on memory to keep cases moving. This puts those firms even further behind those firms that are already weaving AI into their workflows.

AI is unlikely to replace lawyers anytime soon. The practice of law is about judgment, nuance, and emotional intelligence that AI just isn't equipped for. It can't catch the hesitation in a client's voice or decide when to push hard in negotiations versus when to hold back. It can't connect the dots between facts and feelings, between what the law says and what the client actually needs.

The reality is that practicing law, at its core, is a human craft. And lawyers who thrive won't be the ones who try to compete with AI; they'll be the ones who know how to partner with it.

Still, AI isn't magic. And it definitely isn't perfect. Remember when lawyers got sanctioned for submitting briefs filled with fake case law? It's happened often enough that some courts now require certification that a human reviewed anything AI helped create. That alone should tell you everything you need to know: AI is impressive, but it's not infallible.

So no, I'm not saying you should hand your firm over to a machine. What I am saying is this: Learn to use it well. Especially when it comes to building new processes from scratch. It's surprisingly simple, and it saves a ton of time.

Want to see how? Flip to the sidebar on the next page. Even a simple prompt like "List the key steps for..." can give you a working draft of a process in seconds. Use that draft as a conversation starter with your team to turn it into something real.

As I've heard it said more than once, lawyers who use AI well—not to replace their judgment, but to amplify their capacity—will replace the ones who don't. So don't be afraid of change. Embrace it but do it smartly. The future of law isn't artificial. It's intentional.

Quick AI Assist

Feeling stuck? Let AI break the blank-page barrier. You don't need brilliance—just a draft you can refine.

Try prompts like:

- "List the key steps for serving a lawsuit in a personal injury firm."
- "Write a process for how a paralegal should handle client intake after a signed contract."
- "Here's how we do it now [insert description]. Can you turn this into a clear step-by-step workflow with decision points?"
- "Brainstorm five ways to streamline medical records requests for a PI firm."

It won't be perfect. That's not the point. The goal is to get a draft on the page so you and your team can edit, tweak, and finalize it faster.

There's a Process for That

Now that you've seen how processes keep the Client Journey running smoothly, let's turn our attention behind the scenes to the moving parts that hold up the rest of the firm.

Think about what happens when it's time to review financials or schedule an all-hands meeting. If pulling things together involves scattered steps, random tools, or scrambling to figure it out, then you've got an opportunity for a process.

Here are a few areas where a clear, repeatable process can help:

- **Onboarding New Hires:** Give new team members a smooth, consistent start—from training materials to software access.
- **Marketing and Business Development:** Keep outreach efforts steady and effective with processes for newsletters, social media, or lead follow-ups.

- **Billing and Invoicing:** Track time, send invoices, and follow up without missing a beat.
- **Training and Development:** Make growth intentional with processes for CLEs, mentoring, or internal training.
- **Team Meetings and Communication:** Use simple structures to keep meetings focused and follow-ups clear.

Of course, I'm not suggesting you create a process for every little thing. The goal isn't to drown your team in documentation; it's to free them up. Focus on areas where a consistent, repeatable approach saves time, reduces errors, or helps your team work more efficiently. A good rule of thumb? If something keeps coming up and/or is not being handled the same way each time, it probably needs a process.

Set-Up Focus

I know I just took you on a journey into the weird, the uncomfortable, and maybe even the slightly ridiculous. But you came with me anyway—into *Richard's World*, into logic trees and algorithms, into the unseen gears that actually make a firm run.

That matters. Because the truth is, most people don't stop long enough to look at what's underneath their systems or consider what it's costing them not to have one. But you did. You allowed yourself to imagine something different—not just smoother work, but more dignity in the doing of it. More clarity. More care. You didn't treat Process like a box to check. You treated it like it mattered.

So, if I may, I want to push just a little further.

What if this wasn't just about making your firm run better? What if Process is how you show your team—and yourself—that this work is worth doing well? That it deserves structure. That it deserves your full attention—not just in the middle of chaos, but *because* of it. Because when the fires quiet—even for a moment—you have a choice: brace for the next one or start building the systems that keep them from spreading.

Or maybe Process goes deeper than that. Maybe it's about respect. Respect for the time it takes to do something right, for the people doing the work, for the client who's counting on you. Maybe it's not the opposite of freedom, but the foundation of it. Not micromanagement, but trust, made visible. Not red tape, but care, in a form other people can follow.

And maybe, if we're being honest, it goes even deeper than that. Maybe Process is love in the practical tense. Not the lofty, idealized kind, but the kind that files the documents, sends the follow-ups, tracks the deadlines, and gets the work done right the first time. The kind that shows up with clear steps and thoughtful systems so no one has to live in chaos just to prove they're committed.

Because that kind of love—the quiet, structured, ordinary kind—is what creates a firm that people can actually trust. It holds people up. It moves work forward. And it makes room—real breathing room—for the kind of business, and the kind of life, you actually want.

And when the inside of the work is cared for like that, it shows up differently on the outside. That's your Product.

selah

a moment of pause

IN MUSIC, *SELAH* MARKS a pause—a quiet, intentional moment to stop, reflect, and let it all sink in before moving forward.

It's the space between notes, where the weight of what has come before settles. And where the promise of what's ahead begins to take shape. It's a chance to step back, see the whole, and appreciate the journey before returning to the rhythm.

In life, we often need these *selah* moments—a time to step back, look at how far we've come, and refocus on where we're heading. And right now, in the middle of building your firm's Set-Up, it's time for one of those pauses.

I know we've covered a lot of ground already. So let me offer you a word of encouragement.

You see, for the past year, I've been coming into my office every day. My team knows I'm here, but I've been focused on writing this book instead of being in the thick of it with all the things. And yet, the firm hasn't missed a beat. We're still bringing in revenue, still producing a quality Product, still delivering great service to our clients.

But how, without my direct involvement? Because all the pillars of The Set-Up are in place. The Pipeline keeps us on track, our People are committed to our purpose, Process ensures consistency, Product maintains our high standards, and Profitability takes care of itself as a result.

This is the firm I dreamed of when I started, and it's what you're building now. You're here because you want more than just a firm that merely functions. You want a firm that thrives, a firm that means something. You want to know that your team is handling things efficiently, your clients are getting the best possible service, and your firm is profitable—all without requiring the best of you for every detail.

You've already laid a solid foundation with your Pipeline and your People pillars. You've just finished Process, the machinery that ensures everything runs smoothly. And after this, we'll move on to Product and Profitability, rounding out your Set-Up to create a firm that works the way you've always wanted it to.

So, take this moment. The next movement begins soon.

Breathe. Appreciate how far you've come.

Selah.

product

our service

YOU MAY NOT HAVE noticed, but when I introduced the People pillar of The Set-Up, I didn't include our clients. I focused on you as the leader, everyone on your team, and the culture you create around them. But leaving our clients out of the People pillar wasn't an oversight. It was a deliberate decision.

Why?

Because clients aren't just *part* of the world we work in, *they're the whole reason it exists*.

Think about it. Without clients, who are we? Advisors with no one to guide. Advocates with no one to speak for. Fighters with no one to stand beside. It's our clients who give our work meaning. It's their needs that give it weight. Their hope that gives it urgency.

Yet, one of the easiest things to lose sight of is the client.

And with how we're trained, it's no wonder. Law school is like a mental boot camp, shaping us into sharp thinkers. We dissect case law, spot every possible argument, and master the theory inside and out. But they typically leave out one crucial part: the client and their experience as we do all that.

Then we get into practice, and it hits us—real people with real problems—and it takes a while to find our footing. The push and pull of opposing counsel, judges' rulings, and the constant friction of conflict—these things take up our attention. So much so the case becomes a contest of skill instead of a service to someone who's counting on us. We start thinking about the fight, not the person we're fighting for.

And just when we think we've got that lawyering bit down, we decide to start our own firms. Now, it's not just cases and clients, it's payroll, overhead, marketing, and all the moving parts of keeping the doors open. We can't do it all alone, so we hand pieces of the client experience to our staff. But now the client gets passed around, the personal touch fades, and their experience becomes hit or miss.

I don't mean this as an indictment. It happens to all of us. And that's why we couldn't just fit clients into the People pillar and think that was enough. They deserve a space that's all their own; a pillar that honors their place at the center of everything we do. *Product*.

I was reminded of that last June at the Oklahoma Attorneys Mutual Insurance Company's annual board dinner. It's a night I always enjoy—great food, better wine, and even better conversation.

We were giving updates about our firms and our families, while a few grumbled about their golf games. At one point, someone asked what I'd been working on, and I shared about *The Set-Up*. When I described the idea of treating legal work like a "product"—something intentional, consistent, and client-centered—I saw heads nodding.

That's when James, who's been practicing law for over fifty years, leaned back and said, "Back in the day, everything was manual. Carbon paper, dictation, trips to the law library. Then all the tech came along, and we gained so much. But you know what seems to have changed?"

He paused.

"It feels like we lost the *honor* of it all. The *meaning* behind what we do."

That landed like a stone in my chest. Because deep down, I knew exactly what he meant.

At its core, being a lawyer isn't about paperwork, or deadlines, or even the win. It's about the human being behind the case. It's about being a guide and an advocate for someone in one of the hardest moments of their life. It's about stepping in and saying, "I've got you."

That's the spirit of the Product pillar. It's how we remind ourselves why we do this work at all.

In this part, we'll explore what it truly means to center your work around your client's needs. And just as important, we'll talk about how to turn what you do best into something your whole team can deliver—so that every client, every time, gets the experience they deserve.

11

It's All About the Client

The simple act of paying attention
can take you a long way.
KEANU REEVES, *What Keanu Says*

LET'S FLIP the script for a moment.

Think back to the last time you were the client, maybe sitting in a chair for a haircut. You're not wanting a dramatic change, just a refresh, a little shape, something that says "functional adult" instead of "feral raccoon." You explain what you want, maybe even show a picture. The stylist nods and seems to get it.

But twenty minutes later, you're staring at your reflection, thinking, "Is that... *a mullet*?"

Not a bold, ironic mullet. Not a cool Gen Z thing. Just something slightly tragic happening at the back of your head.

And sure, you'll survive. Hair grows. You tell yourself it's not that big of a deal. But that's not what lingers. It's the *feeling* that sticks. Unseen. Ignored. Like your voice didn't carry. Like *you* didn't carry.

Now raise the stakes. But this time, it's not just your hair, it's your legal case. Your life. The thing that keeps you up at night. The thing you finally built up the courage to hand over to someone you thought could help.

And the person sitting across from you—the lawyer you chose, the one you hoped would really listen—keeps glancing at their phone or starts talking over you before you've finished, already laying out what they're going to do about your case. They don't ask what matters most to you; they don't even pause to hear you out. Suddenly, that same sinking feeling comes rushing in. Only this time, the cost isn't a bad haircut. It's your trust.

That's the risk our clients carry when they walk through our doors. They're not just handing over a case. They're handing over a piece of their *life*—a fear, a hope, a chapter they didn't choose but now have to live through. They're trusting us to carry it with care.

And to honor that trust, we have to show up fully—not rushed, not half-listening, not treating their experience like something we've seen a hundred times. (Even if we have.) We have to get out of our own way and make space for the client's full truth: their fears, hopes, values, and all.

Because the better you understand what drives your client, the more effective your representation becomes. Your work gets sharper, more focused, and ultimately more successful. And it starts right there in that moment, sitting across from them, paying full attention, letting them know—not with promises or paperwork, but with presence—"I see you."

The Art of Connection

That kind of I-see-you presence doesn't just come naturally—not for me anyway. I think about when we were getting the firm off the ground. I was so focused on keeping all the balls in the air that *how* I showed up for the client slipped into the background. Survival had just edged everything else out.

And then Jacob joined us.

I still remember sitting in on one of his first client meetings. I was half-listening—probably still fuming over something like opposing counsel's latest outrageous move—when I realized the whole room had gone quiet.

Jacob hadn't said much; he was just... listening. *Really* listening. The client was leaning in, talking in this steady stream you almost never get in a first meeting. The only other thing I could hear was the slight hum of the AC. The client's hands, clenched on the table a moment ago, slowly opened. When they paused, Jacob didn't rush in with advice or a list of next steps. He just said, softly, "*I hear you.* Tell me more about that."

And there was just something about him doing that. You could see the client's shoulders drop, like they'd been holding their breath without knowing it. It was the first time I'd seen an initial client meeting go that deep, that fast.

That moment taught me more about client care than any checklist ever could. Jacob showed us that caring isn't a feeling you have—it's a *skill.* What he did in that room wasn't complicated. He made space. He listened in a way that let the client hand him the truth beneath the facts.

I later learned there's a name for what Jacob was doing: *active listening.*

You've probably experienced the difference this kind of listening makes. Think about two doctors with completely different bedside manners.

The first one barely glances up. They scribble a few notes while you talk, then hand you a prescription with a quick "Here's what you need." You walk out feeling like a footnote in their day. Were they even listening? Did they hear what you were really trying to explain? Maybe you think, "Why did I even bother?"

Now picture a different doctor. This one pulls up a chair, looks you in the eye, and asks, "How long have you been feeling like this?" They actually listen—nodding, repeating some of what you said so you know they got it. They ask questions like "How has this affected your life?" And they give you real space to talk.

Feeling safe, you open up. Maybe you mention that nagging pain you forgot to bring up to the nurse or that family member who's been through something similar. This doctor doesn't rush. They pause, acknowledge your concerns, and offer advice that feels like it's meant for *you.*

So, who do you trust? Which doctor would you come back to? Which one actually made you feel seen? The simple difference between these two doctors? *Active listening*. One did it; the other didn't.

There's nothing complex or mysterious about active listening. But for most of us, it isn't automatic. It takes practice—shutting out everything else, focusing fully on the person in front of you, and listening to understand instead of to respond. This matters because active listening is what creates psychological safety—the kind we talked about when we covered People—a space that's judgment-free, human, and open.

When we give someone that kind of safety, they're far more likely to speak their truth—not just about what happened that brought them to us, but about what they *really* need. Without feeling safe, they might hold back or tell us what they think we want to hear. That leaves us guessing or chasing a solution that doesn't really address the problem. And that kind of disconnect makes our work harder. Weaker. You can't build a great strategy in the dark.

Just like Jacob taught me to genuinely connect with the client to truly understand what they need from us, we have to incorporate active listening into our client work. When we do, we're no longer just gathering facts. We're creating the conditions for the truth beneath the facts to emerge. And once that door opens, what comes through is the thing every client brings us: their *why*.

Active Listening in Practice

Active listening is less about technique and more about making room. It's the quiet pause that lets someone lay down what they've been carrying, the kind of presence that says, "You're safe here." When you practice it, trust grows. Relationships deepen. Conversations open in ways that surprise you, whether you're sitting with a client, standing before a jury, or trying to get your five-year-old to tell you what's really wrong.

To practice active listening:

Remove distractions: Close the laptop, silence the phone, and give your full attention.

Ask open-ended questions: Prompts like "Can you tell me more?" or "What's your perspective?" invite depth.

Listen to understand, not to reply: Pay attention to tone, pauses, and body language, not just words.

Hold the space: Resist jumping in. A pause often uncovers the most important part of the conversation.

Reflect their language: Using their own words back to them shows you heard and valued what they said.

Layer in empathy: A simple acknowledgment like "That sounds like a lot to carry" can shift the whole dynamic.

Keep this list close for client meetings and use it to train your team. Active listening isn't just a legal skill–it's a people skill, and the stronger it gets, the more everything you do benefits.

Your Client's Why

When a new client sits across from you, what they share first is rarely the story that really matters to our work.

They give you their legal issue—the facts—but not the deeper story behind it. Not the thing they most hope for or the cost that keeps them awake all night. They may not even realize that's part of what they need to share.

And that's not their fault. In a moment of crisis, most people aren't thinking about their deeper emotions; they're just trying to get through. When everything feels urgent or overwhelming, the brain goes into survival mode. People focus on the immediate problem in front of them and not the deeper needs underneath.

That's where the risk lives for us as lawyers.

If we build a case solely on the first urgent facts a client shares, we risk missing what really drives the matter. Plus, it's those unspoken pieces that often shape the strongest arguments and clearest path forward. Without them, we're building strategy on a shaky foundation.

And when those pieces come to light too late (or never at all), the cost is high. A claim can be lost. A defense can crumble. The case itself can suffer in ways we can't fix. That's not just a strategic miss; it brushes up against our ethical duty to do the work thoroughly and to truly protect the client's interests. And beneath all of that sits the quiet cost: breaking the trust they placed in us from the start.

That's why we can't build a case on the surface version of the story. We need a way to get underneath it, to uncover what's really driving the case from the start.

What if we had a simple, structured way to help clients talk about what really matters to them? Something that would not only help them articulate what they really need but also give us a way to build strategies that match their real priorities. Then, whatever the matter is—planning for the future, protecting their rights, or fighting their case—we're building a plan rooted in what matters most to the client, one that makes it clear why the outcome we're working toward truly matters to them.

Back in chapter 8, we talked about Simon Sinek's idea of starting with the why—the core purpose that drives people and organizations. While Sinek applies this concept to leaders and teams, I've found it's just as powerful when applied to clients. Because a client's why is the heartbeat of their case, the thing under the facts that gives our whole representation its meaning.

To uncover it, we break the client's why into two parts: mission and vision. Mission is about what your client needs to get through the moment they're in. Vision is about what they hope for once it's behind them. One grounds you in the present; the other points to the future.

Caring isn't a feeling you have—it's a skill you practice.

And when you understand both, you don't just know the details of the case—you know the client. That's when your legal work becomes sharper, more focused, and more aligned with what truly matters.

Your Client's Mission

Your client's mission is their immediate reason for reaching out—the urgent need they can't handle on their own. And in that urgency, what they tell you first is often just the surface.

Sometimes it sounds simple: "I need a divorce," or "I want to be paid what I'm owed." But when you get curious and ask a few deeper questions, their true concern often reveals itself.

A client injured in a car accident might initially say they're worried about medical bills. But with one follow-up—"What's your biggest concern right now?"—you might uncover something much more urgent: "I've missed so much work I'm not sure how I'll pay my mortgage next month." That changes how you frame the strategy and the damages.

Or you might have a client facing workplace discrimination who says they want justice. But when you ask, "What are you most concerned about in how this plays out?," they admit they're terrified of retaliation and losing their job. Their mission isn't just about the claim but about protecting their future.

Understanding the mission helps you avoid making assumptions based on similar cases you handled in the past. You uncover the real stakes—for *this* client—and can build your legal strategy around *their* needs, not just what you assume they want from past experience.

Take two clients with medical malpractice claims. One might be worried about covering immediate expenses from a botched surgery. Another might be focused on protecting a long-standing relationship with their doctor or keeping the matter private. Without digging deeper, you'd never know their true priorities. Exploring each client's mission reveals these individual concerns and keeps you from defaulting to a one-size-fits-all approach.

Catching their mission early doesn't just help you build a better strategy; it protects you from building the wrong one altogether. If you miss what's really at stake for your client, you risk crafting a plan that looks fine on paper but leaves the client unprotected where it matters most.

And remember, clients don't always voice their concerns immediately. After they've explained their issue, follow up with "Is there something else that's worrying you about this?" That one question often opens the door to the fears and motivations they didn't say out loud the first time.

Getting to the mission isn't about having the perfect question—it's about slowing down and listening, so the real concern has room to surface. And once you understand that, you're ready to address their *vision*.

Your Client's Vision

Where mission is about what your client needs now, vision is about what they hope comes next.

Some clients want closure. Others want to send a message or make sure no one else has to go through what they did. Some want to protect their family, their business, or their reputation.

I remember Ed, a client who came to us with a bad faith insurance claim against an insurance company "that shall not be named." (Sorry, a confidentiality agreement prevents me from telling you who it was; just know they're one of the largest spenders on TV.) At first, it seemed like he was just looking for compensation.

But when we pushed a little more, we uncovered a deeper goal. Ed's vision was to hold the company accountable so no one else would be treated the way he had. With that in mind, we secured a settlement that ended the very claims practice that brought him to us.

To uncover this vision, we asked questions like "What do you want to see change after this is behind you?" and "What's the bigger outcome you're hoping for beyond just having the policy limits paid?" These types of questions help clients think beyond their immediate concerns and give you a clearer picture of what they really want in the long run.

Once you understand your client's vision, you can shape your strategy around their long-term goals and head off unrealistic expectations early—like hoping for emotional closure the legal system can't give.

Every client hands over not just a case, but a piece of their life.

Just like with mission, uncovering vision early keeps you from settling a case or structuring relief in a way that technically resolves the claim but misses what the client truly needs.

Strategizing the Why

Now this is where things get good. This is where the client's mission and vision become the backbone of every decision in their case and the framework for your entire strategy—from the first letter you send to the terms of the final documents.

Imagine you're working with a client tangled up in a complex business dispute. Sure, they need immediate protection for their business. But their deeper goal might be preserving the company's reputation. With that in mind, you might skip the courtroom showdown and instead work quietly behind the scenes—to keep the matter private and pursue a resolution that protects relationships, rather than burning every bridge along the way.

Or say you're defending someone charged with DUI. The client needs immediate protection from conviction, yes. But their deeper vision might be preserving their professional license and family stability. They're worried about losing their job, their reputation in the community, and the impact on their children. So, your strategy does both: fights the charges and considers plea options that might avoid professional consequences, explores treatment programs that demonstrate responsibility, and structures any resolution to minimize long-term career and family disruption.

In each matter, you can ask yourself, "How can I meet their immediate need while also setting them up for what comes next?" It's like drawing a line from the present to the future, connecting the dots between today's decisions and the life, business, or outcome they're trying to build. And in that space, you discover more to work with—more context, more clarity, and a fuller picture of what will truly serve them well.

Sometimes, the why is deeply personal.

We once represented a couple who had lost their child due to a defective medication. At first, they just wanted to hold the company accountable. But their vision was bigger: They wanted to set up a foundation in their child's name. Once we understood that, we were able to ensure the settlement supported that vision. It became a way to create meaning from their loss, to honor their child's life, and to make sure that life left a mark long after the case was over.

The point is, when you build your case strategy around the client's why, every choice ties back to what really matters to them. It shapes the case in a way that's human and personal, and that kind of alignment doesn't just move the work forward—it gives it weight. Meaning. It's the kind of lawyering that stays with you long after the file is closed.

It's a Team Sport

Of course, you can't (nor should you) carry this alone. To really keep the client's why at the heart of the work, the whole team has to speak the same language, keeping the client's why front and center in everything they do.

And, yes, this starts with how they listen.

Train your team to go beyond collecting facts; they need to listen for meaning. When a client talks about their accident, their marital separation, their job loss, there's always something beneath the surface. Help your team learn to ask, "What matters most to this person right now?" and listen with that in mind.

During Intake, curiosity is everything. A question like "What's your biggest worry right now?" can uncover what's really going on—not just the surface facts, but the emotional heart of the case. Once that's known, it becomes a guide for how your team shows up, communicates, and builds strategy from that point forward.

Consistency matters. Encourage regular check-ins with questions like "Has anything changed since we last spoke?" Make this a habit—something baked into your Pipeline—so your team stays in sync with what the client needs now, not just what they said at the start.

And teach your team to notice what's *not* being said.

If a client hesitates or suddenly goes quiet, that's not the end of the conversation—it's the beginning of a deeper one. A gentle question like "Is something on your mind?" can open the door to honesty, relief, and trust. These are the moments clients remember—not just being helped but being *held*.

And don't stop at listening.

Make sure every piece of work—motions, briefs, emails—reflects what the client really came to you for: their why. Use language that mirrors their priorities. Frame facts in their context. Be clear. Be direct. Let every choice you make serve the story they need to tell.

When you do that, the client feels the intention and care behind every step you take. That sense of being heard and carried through the process is what they'll remember long after the paperwork is done.

Set-Up Focus

We've all met lawyers who see clients as numbers. To them, cases are just transactions to be pushed through so they can hit their bottom line. Then there are the ones who barely even try. They show up unprepared, with only the faintest grasp of their client's story.

And while it's tempting to roll our eyes and say, "Well, that's not me," the truth is, every time one of those lawyers drops the ball, it chips away at the integrity of what we do.

It's no wonder all those lawyer jokes exist. People laugh at us because, deep down, they don't trust us. They think we care more about our fees than their futures. And while most of us aren't like that, we all carry the weight of the profession's reputation.

But when we strip it all down, it comes to this: We have a choice. We can stay frustrated and defensive about that perception, or we can rewrite it—one client, one case at a time. We can show up differently—for our clients, for our teams, and for ourselves.

Because the practice of law isn't just about nailing the argument or knowing the rules. It's about walking into rooms thick with fear, grief, and hope and choosing to stand with someone in them. It's about sitting across from a person who's carrying something heavy and saying, without words, "I've got you. You're not doing this alone."

That's where the lasting fulfillment in this work comes from. Not the verdicts or the settlements—those fade. It comes from meaning. From service. From knowing you helped someone through the worst chapter of their life and handed them back even a small piece of hope they thought they'd lost.

As I sit here writing this, I keep coming back to those beautifully wise words of Maya Angelou: "...people will forget what you said, people will forget what you did, but people will never forget how you made them feel."

That's what this work is really all about. That's what the Product pillar is really all about. It's not just the outcomes we're able to achieve; it's the experience. It's not just about winning the next big case; it's about making people feel seen and safe at a moment when they need it most. Because in the end, *that's* what they'll remember.

12

A Better Way to Serve

Victorious warriors win first and then go to war, while defeated warriors go to war first and then seek to win.
SUN TZU, *The Art of War*

THERE ONCE was this young lawyer I worked with—let's call her Jamie—who was bright, eager, and ready to jump in. I was in the thick of one of those "whale" cases I mentioned in chapter 3, so I asked her to handle discovery requests for a different case—an underinsured motorist (UM) bad faith matter—so we could keep it moving as discovery deadlines closed in.

Since Jamie didn't know the case details, I pointed her to a set of discovery from a previous case, thinking it would save time.

But that example I pulled was for a property damage bad faith case, not UM.

And in her enthusiasm to get it done, Jamie copied those requests straight into our UM case. She didn't tailor them. She didn't adjust them. So, every request looked like we were handling a roof claim. Questions about material costs, replacement schedules, water leakage—*anything* but what we needed for our UM case. Not a single request asked for proof of the other driver's negligence, our client's medical records, or the details of the accident.

As the busyness of litigation and too much on an already-too-full plate would have it, I didn't review the requests before they went out. I didn't even immediately review the answers when they came in. It wasn't until I finally had the time to get ready for depositions in the case that I pulled the responses. Sick heat rushed through me. Not a single request had been answered. Just snarky objections and dismissive commentary that did nothing to advance the case. Now, we were left needing to turn around and do it all over again.

Yeah, my stomach still drops a little just thinking about it now.

In that moment, my first instinct was to blame Jamie. I mean, it would've been so easy to pin this on her as a rookie mistake. But the truth is, it wasn't about her at all. At the time, I couldn't name what had happened; I just knew it left us fumbling and no closer to moving the case forward.

Later, I'd come to call it "reactive lawyering"—that scramble mode where the work is driven by whatever lands on your desk next: a deadline, a filing, an email, a client call. It's the scramble where your inbox sets the agenda, deadlines drive the day, and the case steers you instead of the other way around. It feels like you're moving fast, but without a clear plan or process, you're just spinning the wheels.

Stop Reacting. Start Strategizing.

You've likely seen it yourself—that frantic pace where the day is nothing but responses and reactivity. It looks like progress in the moment, but without a pre-devised strategy or plan, all that motion isn't moving the case forward. That's reactive lawyering. And if you're not careful, the case (or opposing counsel or an overly enthusiastic client) starts to run you, not the other way around.

So, what's the alternative?

Instead of reacting, what if we built a "box" for our teams—a shared framework that holds our thinking and keeps everyone focused on what truly matters in our cases. One that's in place for every case that walks in the door. One that says: Here's what we're trying to prove. Here's what matters to the client. Here's how this case actually gets won.

This box doesn't restrict—it invites. Structure, when used right, isn't about putting limits on creativity. It's about creating space for the team to be at their best. It supports them by freeing them from the weight of endless decisions and possibilities, helping maintain focus.

Inside the box, the work starts to make sense. The team knows how to shape their efforts, what to prioritize, and how each piece connects to the whole. It gives structure without rigidity—because the contents of the box will change with each client and each case, but the box itself will stay put.

When you work this way, everything connects back to the plan. Motions, depositions, decisions—they all move with intention. Your team understands what matters and why. And when the strategy is clear, the case moves forward with purpose.

This isn't just strategy; it's product thinking. And the best product teams don't wait for things to break; they plan ahead. They study what's gone wrong before, look for patterns, and design solutions that prevent the same issues from happening again.

Of course, law is technically a service profession, but if you really think about it, the result of that service is something tangible. Every case we deliver—every strategy, brief, and resolution—is a product of our thinking. Something built. And like any good product, it should be built with care, tested over time, and improved with experience.

That's what this part of The Set-Up is about.

Pipeline mapped the Client Journey. Process made it efficient. Now Product ties it together so the legal work you deliver is aligned, repeatable, and shaped by what your client truly needs.

In the next few sections, we'll explore three core principles of product development that can elevate how you build your cases and help you lead with strategy, not scramble in reaction. Think of them as the tools that define the "box" you build for your team.

Principle One: If it's a recurring problem, it deserves a permanent solution.

Principle Two: Empowered users are the real measure of great design.

Principle Three: Great products improve continuously.

Principle One

When you see the same problem show up again and again in your clients' cases, pay attention. Recurring issues are signals you might just need to create a permanent fix. Like a product developer, if something keeps breaking, you redesign it until it doesn't.

Take Apple's MacBook keyboards, for instance. After countless complaints about keys getting stuck and repeating characters, Apple realized their butterfly keyboard design wasn't working. They went back to the drawing board and eventually returned to the more reliable scissor-switch mechanism. By looking for a better way to serve, Apple made a strategic move to solve a recurring issue that had become a significant pain point for their users.

Let me give you an idea of how this principle can help.

When I started the firm, we hit a snag pretty quickly. The team was great at digging up every possible fact and knew the law inside out. But when it came to putting it all together for our clients' cases, things got messy.

We had tons of facts, but not all of them mattered. And without a story to frame them, by the time we got to strategy—prepping key depositions or trial—we were scrambling to pull it together, especially when it came to the facts that didn't favor us.

That's why we built a process ("a box," as it were) that gets us thinking strategically from the moment a case comes in. We call it our Case Narrative, and it's built around six key questions drawn from a blend of best practices I've encountered through books, a trial school I attended, and a bit of my own approach.

Here's the full process, with the questions and the thinking behind each one, so you can see how the structure works in practice:

Control doesn't create consistency— structure does.

1 **What happened?** This simple question is the foundation of our Case Narrative. By focusing only on the most relevant facts of the event that brought our client to us, we're doing more than collecting evidence—we're crafting the framework of the story, cutting through the noise to highlight the essential details that will shape the outcome we're aiming for.

And on this point, I have a silly phrase I use with my team: "You have to be willing to give up sexy." They know exactly what I mean. Even if you've got a flashy fact that sounds great, if it doesn't serve the story, it doesn't make the cut.

2 **Why shouldn't it have happened?** Here, we zero in on the specific actions—or lack of actions—that led to the problem. We identify the mistakes, but, more importantly, the clear choices that caused our client's harm. Maybe it was a driver who chose to run a red light or a company that ignored repeated requests for assistance. By focusing on these specific failures, we show how the harm could have been avoided if the right choices had been made.

3 **What are the rules?** Grounding our case in the rules—whether statutes, case law, jury instructions, or industry norms—gives structure to the Case Narrative. But this is more than simply citing the rules. We actually weave them into the narrative we're shaping. This way we're focused on the facts that demonstrate where those standards were breached. This ensures that we highlight only the facts that strengthen the case. Everything else gets cut.

4 **Why do you think it happened?** This is where we explore the defendant's motivation. Not what they say—but what we believe drove their behavior. Were they rushing? Cutting corners? Prioritizing profit over safety? This gives shape to their decisions in a way that's consistent with the facts and connects their choices to the consequences.

5 **Why do they say it happened (or didn't)?** This step forces us to anticipate the opposition. What's their version of the story? Their justification? Their likely spin? Instead of waiting to respond, we fold that perspective into our strategy from the beginning—preparing

our counterpoints, reinforcing our own framing, and inoculating the case against surprises.

6 **What was the result?** Finally, we return to the client. What was the impact of what happened—emotionally, physically, financially? This is where damages become human again. The point here is to go beyond the special damages (those economic harms we can calculate to a number). It's about what was lost, what changed, and why this case matters. It's about grounding the entire strategy in the client's why.

Our Case Narrative kicks off right at Intake, with our team beginning a unique narrative for each client by working through these foundational questions. The Case Narrative then guides every decision we make on the case—from drafting the initial pleading to determining the evidence we need and the legal approach we'll take.

And as the case progresses, our Case Narrative isn't static. It adapts and sharpens with each new detail, informing everything from summary judgments to depositions and guiding us in selecting expert witnesses. By the time we reach trial prep, we're not scrambling for an opening statement or second-guessing what evidence proves our case; we've been working on it and actually thinking about it since day one.

Putting this into a process has saved hours of wasted effort on irrelevant discovery. It's created consistency across cases. It's given new attorneys a built-in way to think like seasoned lawyers. It's helped experienced team members stay focused when things get hectic.

But maybe most importantly, it has allowed me to step back. Because once the team understood the Case Narrative, I no longer had to be in every meeting or approve every move. The case strategy—the one best practices call for—is already baked into the case and the team is thinking through every question from the moment the case starts. It's like I transferred years of legal experience and judgment—my "intellectual property," if you will—into a process the entire firm can use. Now, I can focus on the firm itself—growth, leadership, culture—while knowing the cases are still being built with the same care and intentionality I'd bring myself.

So, think about your firm. What challenges do you keep running into? Is your team over-prepping weak facts? Are strategies changing from case to case? Are you doing too much yourself? Wherever you feel friction, there's a chance to build structure. The more you turn recurring challenges into repeatable wins, the stronger your Product becomes.

Takeaway: Recurring issues are design opportunities. When you spot a friction point, don't just patch it. Build around it.

Principle Two

In product development, the best designs make users feel confident and capable right from the start.

Think about the set-up experience for a new iPhone. It's intuitive, welcoming, and designed so anyone can unbox it and get started right away. And really, when was the last time you bought a product that didn't come with some kind of user manual?

That's exactly what we want for our clients. We want them to see the case clearly, understand the standards that apply, and step into their role with confidence. When they can do that, they stop feeling like spectators and become true partners in the work.

Here's one example of how we put that into practice. In our bad faith cases, we noticed clients often struggled to understand the legal standards their insurer was supposed to meet and had a hard time explaining what went wrong in a way that tied back to the heart of the case. We needed a way to make those principles visible and usable—something simple that would anchor their understanding and strengthen their voice.

I'd been familiar with *Rules of the Road* by Rick Friedman and Patrick Malone since early in my practice. Their emphasis on grounding cases in clear legal principles that juries can easily grasp sparked an idea: What if we gave our clients the same clarity? Out of that came what we call our Bad Faith Triangle, a straightforward visual that breaks down the three overall duties insurers must meet and helps clients pinpoint exactly where those duties were breached.

The Bad Faith Triangle

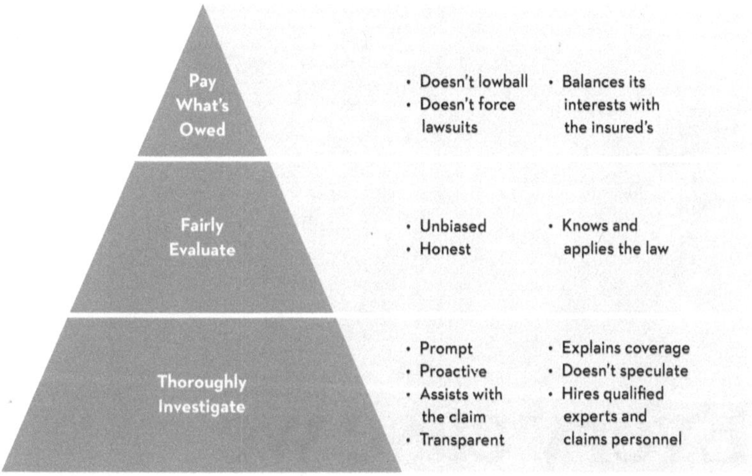

We also built an internal process to share the triangle with clients during Intake and deposition prep. By putting the standards into a simple, tangible framework, clients not only gain a good overview of the legal principles that drive their case but are also able to engage in their case with real understanding.

Take Anne, for instance. She was deposed in her bad faith case against a defendant we'll call ABC Insurance Company. In a typical deposition, she might have been asked, "So, what exactly did ABC Insurance Company do wrong?" Without context, most clients hesitate or fumble through an answer. But since Anne had seen the triangle and understood the duties at stake—to investigate thoroughly, communicate honestly, and settle fairly—she was ready.

When that question came, she responded clearly and confidently:

> ABC Insurance Company didn't fully investigate my claim—they dismissed evidence of my injuries and never contacted my witnesses. They also failed to explain why they were lowballing my settlement, and they refused to consider the extent of my damages . . . even after I provided medical records and gave them a recorded statement. They just ignored their responsibility to settle my claim fairly.

Every case we deliver—every strategy, brief, and resolution—should be built with care.

Well done, Anne!

And this wasn't just a scripted answer—it was Anne's own words, grounded in a clear understanding of the legal standards. That's the real power of a tool like this. It gives clients a way to see their case, speak to it, and step into it with authority.

Your clients may not be in bad faith cases, but the principle holds—whether they are family law clients navigating "best interests of the child" or criminal defense clients needing to understand mitigating factors. When you create simple tools that give them clarity, you build stronger cases and stronger client trust at the same time.

Takeaway: Well-informed clients speak with confidence and credibility. Give them tools that let them see the heart of their case and speak to it with authority.

Principle Three

Product developers don't stop once they've launched a product; they constantly gather feedback—through surveys, reviews, and usage data—and refine their products to stay relevant to users' needs.

Take Netflix, for example. It started with red envelopes and DVDs in the mailbox. Remember that? But as technology shifted and users' habits changed, Netflix didn't dig in its heels—it pivoted. Streaming became the future. And by meeting people where they were headed instead of where they'd been, Netflix turned a fading rental model into one of the world's most dominant platforms.

In the same way, gathering and using feedback throughout your case development helps you to serve clients better over time. When client feedback is built into your Product, you're always fine-tuning and improving.

For example, you might start gathering real-time feedback at key moments on the Client Journey. After an initial consultation, for instance, you could ask, "Was everything clear?" or "Did this process meet your expectations?" Hearing from clients at these points helps you spot common themes.

Maybe you'll find that clients really appreciate knowing the timeline for each major stage in their case. With that insight, you can create a visual roadmap of your Pipeline—something you can hand to clients to show what each stage involves and what's coming next. It gives clients a better sense of progress, grounding them in the process and building confidence as they move forward.

The cases themselves offer valuable feedback, as well. Reviewing both successful outcomes and those that fell short allows you to see where adjustments might sharpen your team's focus, thereby strengthening future cases.

Say, for example, your firm handles immigration asylum cases. After reviewing several cases, you notice a pattern: Cases with compelling personal narratives and clear documentation consistently have stronger outcomes. So, you adjust your process: focus on story collection during Intake and secure corroborating evidence early. Suddenly, every case gets stronger.

Involve your team, too. Set up regular post-case debriefs or monthly review sessions where the team shares what's working and what could be improved. Debriefs foster creativity and hone your team's skills. What's more, you create a cycle of shared learning and improvement across the board.

So, think of where you might incorporate feedback as an essential part of your Product pillar. Your team will build stronger skills, and your clients will feel a deeper sense of trust and value.

Takeaway: The best legal services evolve through feedback. Create systems to learn from each case so your approach gets sharper over time.

Set-Up Focus

There's a moment every law firm owner hits: the quiet fear that if you're not in the middle of every single detail, everything will fall apart. I lived there for years. If a client called, I wanted my hands on the file before anyone else touched it. If a case was moving into discovery, I wanted to personally take every deposition. I told myself it was about quality. But if I'm honest, it was about control.

What I didn't realize back then was that control doesn't create consistency—structure does. When you stop working in reaction mode and start thinking in terms of structure, the weight of it all is no longer on you alone. When your team understands the best practices for building a case and starts with the same playbook, you're no longer carrying the whole thing on your back.

That's what Product gives you: a box that holds the thinking, not just the tasks. Once you've built the process that carries that box, the system itself does the heavy lifting. Your role evolves. You get to choose: Be the coach who sets the vision and shapes the team; run your own cases, if that's where you thrive; or focus on growing the business, if that's where you're needed most.

There's freedom in that box. Not because it takes you out of the work, but because it anchors the work so securely that you're no longer the glue. When the system is built well, it creates confidence for everyone—for your team, for your clients, and for you.

Even if it's just you and a paralegal right now, don't wait to build it. Start small: Write down the three things every case must answer—what happened, why it matters, and how you'll prove it. That's the foundation of your box. Then create a process that carries it, let the system hold the weight, and give yourself room to lead instead of struggle. Because when the weight shifts off your shoulders and the work anchors in the system, something else shifts, too. Your Profitability.

profitability
our results

HOW MANY OF YOU picked up this book and were tempted to flip straight to the part on Profitability?

I don't blame you. Profit is a powerful motivator—and one of the toughest challenges we face as law firm owners. It's also what makes a business sustainable.

Now, if you're expecting this part to be about spreadsheets or profit and loss (P&L) statements, don't worry—it's not. Yes, those tools matter, and every business owner should understand their numbers. But that's not where we're going.

Those things are useful, but they're tactical. What we're talking about here is something more foundational. It's about building a business where profit isn't an afterthought—it's part of the structure. Where every decision supports long-term financial health, not just short-term wins.

You don't need a finance degree to build that kind of firm. You might just need a new way of thinking.

I did.

In the early years of building my firm, Profitability wasn't my focus. I was so in love with the work we were doing and proud that we were doing it differently, making a profit felt like an afterthought—like the great-aunt you've heard about but never actually met.

I believed that if we stayed focused on People, Pipeline, Process, and Product, profit would follow. And to a degree, it did, because we saw some positive financial results. But the kind of stability I was craving—the kind that funds growth, cushions hard seasons, and lets you exhale—always felt just out of reach. We'd make progress, then backslide. The cycle of feast and famine kept repeating. And I didn't know how to stop it.

So, I turned to the usual advice. Cut costs. Bring in more cases. I even restructured attorney compensation, thinking that tying pay to outcomes would speed up the Pipeline and boost our cash flow. But none of these delivered the breakthrough I needed. The team felt undervalued, and money was still tight. And we were working harder than ever without the financial breathing room to show for it.

Eventually, I had to admit it: I wanted profit, but I wasn't *building* it. I was waiting for it to show up instead of giving it a pillar of its own.

So, we changed that.

We went back to the foundation and gave Profitability a seat at the table—just like the other pillars—with its own structure, systems, and strategy. We strengthened the existing pillars. We started tracking performance. We adopted Profit First principles that we'll talk more about in chapter 15. We gave every dollar a job. And we started asking a new question: Does this support the firm's long-term financial health?

The results were transformative. Within a year, our revenue doubled. Not because of a windfall case, but because of small strategic decisions compounding over time. Since then, we've doubled our revenue again—and again.

Maybe you're already focused on profit. Or maybe you're still just trying to keep the lights on. Either way, the upcoming chapters are here to help you make Profitability foundational.

Because Profitability isn't the prize you get at the end. It's what shows up when everything else is working the way it should. When your People, Pipeline, Process, Product, and Profitability pillars are aligned, profit lasts. It's why I've come to think of Profitability less like a reward and more like a quiet kind of readiness.

That's the kind of Profitability we're after.

13

Investing in People

My Precious...
GOLLUM, *The Fellowship of the Ring*

LAST SUMMER on my way into the office, I was listening to the radio. I usually just tune it out, as I'm thinking about what's on board for the day. But somewhere in the background, a discussion caught my attention. The topic was job growth challenges after the COVID-19 pandemic. "The Great Resignation," they called it.

It got me thinking. In business, growth is almost always focused on numbers—metrics, profits, market expansion. And in the law firm world, talk of growth is typically about how many cases your firm is handling, how many new team members you've added, or how many new offices you've opened. But what about the human side of things? It seems we measure every victory except whether our team feels victorious.

If the Great Resignation has taught us anything, it's that numbers aren't the whole story. We know our people are precious, but when we neglect investing in them—or get too busy to focus on it—the costs show up everywhere: low morale, high turnover, declining work quality, and ultimately, reduced profitability.

That's why any strategy for Profitability has to be rooted in human-centered growth. After all, it's not just us—it's them! When we take this perspective, we build happier, more engaged teams, and that brings higher productivity, more creativity, and, yes, better results.

The numbers back it up.

Gallup shows that highly engaged teams see a 21 percent increase in profits. That's no small bump. Deloitte puts that number even higher—companies that prioritize the employee experience are four times more profitable than those that don't. And McKinsey & Company calls talent the "secret sauce" for business success.

So how do you actually do this? Over the years, we've found that a few simple, consistent approaches have helped our team grow—not just as professionals, but as human beings. And that growth fuels better results for everyone.

Why Talk About Team Growth Here?

When I first wrote this chapter, I thought it belonged in the *People* section. That felt right to me—after all, leadership, mission, culture, *and* team development all start with people.

But as I looked more closely at our own experience and dug deeper into the research, I realized something important: Developing your team isn't just a "people thing." It's a foundational business strategy. And one of the smartest, most reliable ways to drive growth.

So, I moved the chapter. Not just because it fits here, but because it belongs here. Because it makes the point unmistakable.

People who grow, perform. It's that simple. And when your team grows, so does your firm.

Strategic Continuous Learning

As a lawyer, you probably know the CLE scurry. That end-of-year dance when you realize you're short on hours, so you start grabbing whatever classes you can—helpful or not, interesting or not. It's not exactly inspiring. More like checking a box so you can move on. And let's be honest—*yuck*.

But what if continuing education didn't feel like a chore? What if it became a lever for growing your team and strengthening your firm?

In the business world, this is called "strategic continuous learning." I call it being intentional with a purposeful, long-term approach to growing talent based on what the firm actually needs to succeed. Instead of chasing needed hours, you invest in learning that moves the firm forward.

For us, that means doubling down on our core practice areas. We handle a high volume of trucking cases, so our attorneys don't just take generic litigation CLEs. Instead, they go to CLEs focused solely on the trucking industry—its regulations, its pain points, and its language. When our lawyers come back from those courses, they're more confident, sharper, and better equipped. More importantly, they're spotting issues and making arguments they would have missed with generic training.

The same goes for our traumatic brain injury cases. When we attend CLEs and seminars focused on mTBIs, we're learning how to spot signs others miss—the subtle symptoms, the tests that matter (and those that don't), and why juries so often misunderstand these injuries. We've since built a checklist of key neurological symptoms to screen for during Intake so that we're asking the right questions from day one. That kind of focus comes straight from strategic CLEs.

But what really makes this investment stick is that we don't keep it siloed.

After every CLE, our attorneys share what they've learned in team debriefs. We fold new ideas into our workflows and update processes accordingly. In essence, learning becomes a firm-wide strategy instead of one person's notebook on a shelf.

When strategic learning becomes part of the culture, people don't just stay. They rise. They bring new energy. They elevate the work. That's the difference between taking CLEs for the sake of hours and learning with a strategic purpose in mind. Because when your people grow, your firm can't help but grow, too.

So, if you aren't doing it already, make sure your CLE choices align with your clients' needs, and then make space to debrief with your team. That's how learning becomes strategy.

Making Growth Part of the Job

Strategic continuous learning isn't just for lawyers; it applies to everyone. Some of the best investments you'll ever make in your firm don't show up on a balance sheet. They show up in people: what they learn, how they grow, and what they bring back to the work.

Here are a few ways to build growth into everyday work and into your profitability strategy.

Tailored Training Opportunities: Support paralegals in pursuing certifications. Pay for specialized legal workshops. Align learning with roles *and* firm strategy.

Cross-Training: Let legal assistants shadow paralegals or paralegals get familiar with Intake and Operations. Flexibility strengthens resilience.

Project-Based Learning: Invite staff to join marketing efforts, operations updates, or strategy meetings. Broaden their perspective, and in turn, your team's creativity.

Mentorship Programs: Pair experienced staff with newer team members. It builds trust and transfers institutional knowledge in a personal way.

Support for Further Education: When someone pursues a degree or professional certification, support them where you can. You'll be remembered as part of their story.

Regular Skills Sharing: Host casual "lunch-and-learn" sessions where team members share something new. A quick insight could spark the next big idea.

Work-Life Balance

At my previous firm, I worked with two associates. One was highly experienced and delivered great results without burning the midnight oil. The other was new and still gaining confidence, so logged long hours to compensate. The managing partner often praised the one who stayed late, using them as the benchmark for everyone else.

Watching it unfold, I was incredibly frustrated. I knew what each brought to the table, and just because one logged more hours didn't mean they added more value. Especially in a contingency-fee practice like ours, where it's not about how many hours you log, but what those hours produce.

By the time I started my firm in 2014, I was already questioning the traditional eight-to-five model. I'd heard of a few businesses experimenting with more flexible approaches, and I figured, why not try it? Aside from our intake specialist (someone's got to answer the phones), everyone could set their own schedule. We could also drop traditional paid time off (PTO). Instead of tracking hours off, we'd encourage people to take time when they need it.

And we built systems to support that flexibility. With our Pipeline, Process, and Product, our team knows what success looks like and how to deliver it. They stay so focused and engaged, sometimes I find myself reminding them it's okay to unplug and reset.

Years later, when I read Cal Newport's book *Slow Productivity*, it felt like a giant yes. He put into words what I had already started to suspect back then: The real path to results isn't nonstop hustle, but focused, sustainable effort. You don't have to work more hours to get results; you just have to work smarter.

A *Harvard Business Review* survey found that companies offering true flexibility see higher engagement and productivity. Another study in the *Journal of Applied Psychology* found that when employees feel trusted, job satisfaction and commitment go up. So, when you give your team flexibility, you're giving your firm a gift.

And, yes, putting people first ties directly to Profitability. When people are burned out, they don't just feel worse; they work less effectively.

They make more mistakes, so your productivity slows down. Some people get so fed up they just walk away. All of that costs money.

But when your team feels trusted and supported, their work improves. They think more clearly, solve problems faster, and stay longer. For contingency-fee firms, that leads to stronger outcomes and faster case resolution.

And for firms that bill by the hour, it matters just as much.

Because if you're billing by the hour, the pressure is always there to bill *more*. But what if each hour billed was worth more because the person behind it was rested, focused, and fully engaged?

That lawyer writes a tighter brief. Spots the issue faster. Handles the call with more clarity and patience. They waste less time circling the answer and deliver more value in less time. When your team is working this way, they don't just do better work. They can handle *more* work. They're no longer losing hours to exhaustion, indecision, or rework. That's where real profitability comes from.

Here's how to start:

- **Shift focus from hours to outcomes.** Track what's being *accomplished*, not just what's being logged.
- **Build in flexibility where you can.** Let team members adjust their start and end times or work remotely a few days a week.
- **Normalize time off.** Model it yourself. Make space for rest without guilt.
- **Trust, but check in.** Autonomy doesn't mean zero structure—just clearer expectations and more respect for how people meet them.

If even one of these shifts feels doable, try it. You don't have to overhaul everything. Just start with a single change and watch the ripple effects.

Honestly? In all the years we've run this way, I can count on one hand the number of times someone took "too much" time off. And even then, it was a blip. When you treat people like adults, they usually rise to the occasion. They take care of their work—and of themselves.

The smartest growth strategy starts from the inside out:
Develop your people.

Because when people feel supported, they perform better. And when your people perform better, your firm thrives.

The Real Cost of Losing Someone

When a good team member walks out the door, it doesn't just sting emotionally; it dents your wallet. Replacing them can cost anywhere from *half to twice their salary*.

And that's not counting the brain drain, the delay in getting things done, or the fact that you're back in the hiring game again.

But it's more than just hiring. It's the time it takes to train someone new. The things that fall through the cracks while you're short-staffed. The quiet dread that maybe someone else is thinking of leaving, too.

So, if you're thinking that investing in your people costs too much... just wait until you see the bill for *not* investing in them.

Monday Morning Meetings

Meetings! Ugh! If you're like me, you probably think most meetings are a waste of time. What actually gets said could usually be covered in an email—and done with less eye-rolling. But some meetings really do matter. And for us, one of those is our Monday Morning Meeting.

We call them MMMs (I know, very original). But they've become sacred at our firm.

MMMs aren't your typical boring meetings with everyone focused on casework or legal briefings. Instead, they're about something far bigger: *growth*. Individual growth, team growth, culture-building kind of growth, our collective and individual growth. MMMs are how we start the week with intention and keep our values front and center.

We've explored ideas from books like Adam Grant's *Hidden Potential*, Brené Brown's *Dare to Lead*, James Clear's *Atomic Habits*, and Cy

Wakeman's *No Ego*. These sessions spark conversations about leadership, mindset, collaboration, and how we show up for each other.

Sometimes we dig into practical topics like time management, storytelling, or active listening—tools we use daily. Other times, it's all about revisiting our core values and asking: "How do we actually live these out in our work?"

And then there are Third Mondays.

On the third Monday of every month, we do something special. It's become a favorite across the team—a simple but powerful framework that brings depth and connection. Each team member shares updates across six topics:

1. **Success:** Celebrate a win but make it about someone else. This builds a culture of appreciation and recognition that flows from peer to peer, not just top-down.
2. **Gratitude:** Share something you're thankful for, big or small. It keeps us grounded and reminds us of the good.
3. **Challenge:** Name a hurdle you're facing. It opens the door for support, problem-solving, or just listening. Vulnerability builds trust.
4. **Personal Update:** Life happens outside of work. This is space to share milestones, hobbies, or anything meaningful going on outside the office.
5. **Needs/Leads/Reads:** Ask for help. Offer a resource. Recommend a book, podcast, or show that's inspiring or just plain fun. It's connection beyond the case file.
6. **Accountability:** What did you commit to last time? What progress have you made? This is gentle, supportive accountability that helps us stay aligned with what matters most.

In an industry known for high pressure and burnout, our MMMs are a reminder that people come first. They've become a core part of our culture and a key reason our team is engaged, supported, and successful. Yet they're more than a cultural bonus, they're also a retention and performance strategy. When people are heard, seen, and connected, they stay, and they perform.

You don't need to copy our format exactly. But what if your weekly meeting became a tool for building trust, deepening connection, and investing in your team's growth? It may sound "soft," but it's actually a strategy that delivers real results. And in the long run, it's one of the smartest investments you can make for your people—and your profitability.

Set-Up Focus

Investing in people is tender work. It's not like buying software or upgrading your office space. You're pouring into human beings—into their dreams, their skills, their futures. And there's a part of you that knows, no matter how much you give, they might take all of that growth and walk away someday.

That's the part that stings. That quiet late-night fear: *What if I give them everything and they leave?* It's tempting to hold them close, to protect your investment like Gollum clutching his ring. But that kind of possessiveness kills the very thing you're trying to nurture.

I've sat with that question. I've let it keep me up. And I've learned to accept they just might. Your investment might make them even more desirable to someone else. But when people leave carrying your firm's values with them, that's not a loss. That's legacy.

And that's exactly why you choose to do it anyway. Because the only thing riskier than pouring into people who may go is not investing in the ones who stay. A team that isn't growing doesn't hold steady; it slowly sinks. And before you know it, you're not building a firm, you're managing its decline.

So, you choose the risk. You invest anyway. You pour into their growth, their well-being, their ability to thrive—not just because it's good business (though it is), but because it's the right thing to do. When you invest in your people, the firm takes on a different heartbeat. The work takes on a different heartbeat. There's no denying it. A team that feels seen and supported shows up differently. They carry the mission. And they care about the work as much as you do.

So, as you look for ways to build a stronger team, remember: This isn't just about today. It's about creating the kind of firm that endures. A team that's skilled and supported performs better. A team that feels seen and valued sticks around. And a culture built on excellence becomes the engine of long-term Profitability.

14

Measure It and It Will Come

It is not enough to be busy; so are the ants. The question is: What are we busy about?
HENRY DAVID THOREAU, *The Journal of Henry David Thoreau*

WHEN WE CRAFTED our Pipeline and Process, we knew we were onto something special. We had taken the chaos of the traditional yet unstructured law firms we'd all come from and created an organized and efficient calm out of the noise. After suffering through a few years without steady financial outcomes, though, I kept thinking about that line whispered to Kevin Costner's character in *Field of Dreams*.

(You know the one. I'd say it, but let's not tempt the copyright fates.)

Costner plays Ray Kinsella, a farmer who hears a mysterious voice in his cornfield. Instead of brushing it off as delusion, he listens. And he builds a baseball diamond right in the middle of his crops. Everyone thinks he's lost it. But he does it anyway.

With that same kind of wild faith, we built something we felt in our bones we had to create: our law firm. And, yes, there were plenty of naysayers out there. Folks who doubted we could find success on our own. But we did it anyway. We put together an incredible team of People, created a Pipeline humming with clients and cases, nailed down our Process, and fine-tuned our Product.

Yet, despite all of that, there was still an ever-elusive missing piece. We had built it, so where was the reward? Profitability had to be there somewhere. But where? I tore through the numbers. I circled the Pipeline like a hawk. I paced at midnight, trying to see what I'd missed. Where was it? Where was it hiding?

And then one night, staring at the same spreadsheets I'd been staring at for years, it hit me: Chasing the numbers wasn't the answer. The truth had been right in front of me all along. It's just that being the stubborn gal I am, it took me a while to admit it: I wasn't measuring the right things in the right way. I wasn't using key performance indicators (KPIs) to guide our way.

You see, I'd heard about KPIs before—in masterminds, in books—but I always tuned them out. Numbers felt cold, mechanical, too far from the human side of running a firm. So, I'd ignored them. Yet, when nothing else had cracked the code, I finally gave in and built KPIs tied to our People, Pipeline, Process, Product, and Profitability.

And like all of us stubborn folks who are a little too hardheaded for our own good, I'd been wrong to ignore them all that time. Profitability wasn't hiding at all. It was standing right there, waving a flag. Because once we started measuring what mattered, it didn't just show up—it strutted onto the field like it had been waiting on us all along.

Took me long enough. But, like I said, I'm stubborn.

What and Why of KPIs

Okay, I know KPIs might sound intimidating, like some big business thingamajig lawyers have no use for. And honestly, that's partly because of how they're usually described.

Business expert David Parmenter calls KPIs the measures that "tell management how the organization is performing 24/7, daily, or weekly in their critical success factors, and by taking action, management is able to increase performance dramatically."

See what I mean? Useful? Absolutely. But it's also the kind of language that can make a law firm owner's eyes glaze over, like it belongs in a Fortune 500 boardroom, not a practice juggling depositions and Intake calls. And this was the simplest explanation I could find!

Strip away the corporate jargon, though, and KPIs are beautifully simple. They're just a handful of metrics that tell you if your firm is breathing easily or gasping for air. They're quick pulse checks that show you what's thriving, what's struggling, and what needs attention.

And the part I love? They cut through all the noise.

Think of them as questions a good friend would ask when they can tell you're about to run yourself off a cliff: Are you sleeping? Are you eating? Do you maybe need to slow down before you faceplant onto your desk at 3:00 p.m.?

That's what KPIs do for your business. They hold up the mirror. They say, "Here's where you are right now. Here's what's actually happening under the surface. Do you want to do something about it before it gets worse?"

When you use them well, the impact is immediate. They make it clear what each person should focus on day-to-day, whether it's following up with clients, closing cases faster, or responding to leads. When your team knows exactly what's being tracked and how it connects to the firm's overall success, they step up. They take action sooner, pay closer attention to details, and work more consistently.

KPIs also help you spot problems early before they become costly. Say you're tracking how many five-star Google reviews you get each month. If that number suddenly drops, it's a warning sign. Maybe clients aren't getting timely updates, or cases are taking too long to resolve. Whatever the issue, the data tells you something's off so you can fix it before it turns into a lost referral or a damaged reputation.

And it's not just about catching problems. KPIs spotlight what's working, too. They give you proof: when to hire, where to invest, and what to double down on. They create a cycle of continuous improvement, where small strategic tweaks add up to big growth over time.

That's how great firms grow—not in one dramatic leap, but through consistent, intentional progress. Within the first year of adopting KPIs, our Profitability doubled. Yes, doubled—because I knew where things were stalling. And then it doubled again over the next several years. Now I have a slightly different take on that iconic *Field of Dreams* line: "Measure it, and it will come."

In the next sections, I'll share some of the KPIs we use and how you can start building your own. The key is starting small and focusing on metrics that directly connect to your five pillars.

A Simpler Way to Measure What Matters

KPIs can feel heavy. I've seen a dozen different systems, each one more complicated than the last, and none of them felt practical for a busy law firm.

So, I pared it back to what actually works. This is a simple approach we use in our firm. It's easy to remember, easy to follow, and—most importantly—easy to put into action.

KPIs Made Simple

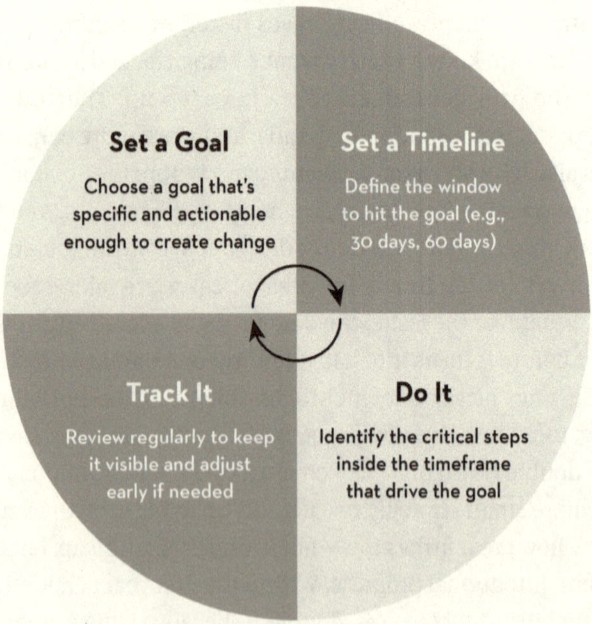

KPIs show you where you are— so you can figure out where to go next.

Pipeline KPIs

We started our journey of using KPIs with our Pipeline.

We did this because it's where I could see our cases stalling. When cases stall, it not only is frustrating for clients, but also impacts our financial health, as revenue only comes in when cases cross the finish line.

So, we examined the Pipeline, looking for those Pipeline Objectives where timeliness seemed to be a recurring issue—the things that created bottlenecks slowing us down. We then established KPIs focused on specific timeframes within which the team needed to accomplish those Objectives.

You might think of these KPIs as our way of accelerating our "product development" timeline. With these benchmarks in place, we began diligently tracking our progress to ensure we stayed on course.

We started with our 80% Team, which handles cases we believe to be most likely to settle without ever stepping into a courtroom.

Our Stage One KPIs here look like this:

Stage One KPIs

1 **Set a Goal**	2 **Set a Timeline**	3 **Do It**	4 **Track It**
Speed up settlement timeline Benchmark: Demands sent in 60 days	60 days from end of treatment to demand sent	Medical coordinator completes file in 45 days Lawyer drafts and sends demand 14 days later	Monitor in CMS Weekly check-ins

First, we made a goal. We wanted to speed up the case settlement timeline so clients weren't left waiting and our cash flow stayed steady. To make that outcome specific and actionable, we set a benchmark: Send every demand to the insurance company within sixty days of the client finishing treatment.

Then, we set a timeline to reach that goal: We defined the KPI window as sixty days from the end of treatment to the demand being sent. That gave us a clear, consistent way to measure whether we were hitting the goal.

Next, we did it. Inside that sixty-day window, two key actions drive the goal: the medical coordinator completing the medical file within forty-five days and the lawyer finalizing and sending the demand within the next fourteen days (with one "cushion" day added in). Those steps became the lever to hit the larger outcome.

Finally, we tracked it. We built the deadlines into our CMS and Pipeline dashboard and review them regularly so we can adjust early and keep cases moving.

The 80% Team meets weekly for a quick check-in. They discuss how things are going, share any challenges, and make sure everyone is aligned on goals and timelines. This routine keeps everyone motivated and cases moving smoothly. And when they move smoothly, the revenue hits our trust account in a timely manner.

Stage One KPIs gave our team clear expectations and a tangible connection between timelines and outcomes. It turned something that used to feel vague—"let's get the demand out"—into something focused and trackable.

Now let's talk about Stage Two—our Litigated Cases. At first, I didn't think we could set reliable KPIs here, since so much is out of our hands when we're litigating a case. I mean, there are defense counsel's stall tactics, the timing of a judge's decisions, witness and trial schedules, you name it.

But instead of focusing on what we couldn't control, we decided to focus on what we *could*.

Stage Two KPIs

1 **Set a Goal**	2 **Set a Timeline**	3 **Do It**	4 **Track It**
Keep Litigated Cases moving Benchmark: Resolve discovery deficiencies in 30 days	30 days from date responses received to resolution	24 hours: Check documents 2 weeks: Review and send deficiency letter 1 week after letter: Meet and confer 2 weeks after meet and confer: Motion to compel, if needed	Monitor in CMS Weekly check-ins

We made a goal: Resolve discovery deficiencies within thirty days of receiving the defendant's responses to written discovery. This helped us keep cases moving without letting common delays derail our progress.

Then, we set a timeline for the steps needed to reach that goal. This included clear deadlines:

- Twenty-four hours to check that all documents came with the written discovery
- Two weeks to review discovery responses and send a deficiency letter, if needed
- One week after sending the letter to schedule a "meet and confer"
- Two additional weeks to file a motion to compel, if necessary

Next, we did it: Our team follows these deadlines with built-in accountability measures. Paralegals flag any missing documents immediately and route cases to attorneys for review according to the timeline. If we need to send a deficiency letter, we use our standardized templates to maintain consistency.

Finally, we tracked it: All these deadlines are integrated into our CMS, and our Stage Two paralegals monitor progress and nudge team members, when needed. This way, if a Litigated Case stalls in Stage Two, it won't be because of something we had control over.

Stage Two KPIs not only gave us back some control in the middle of what can often feel chaotic but also created consistency. And that consistency, over time, helped move cases forward and protect the revenue in our Pipeline, keeping the financial rhythm steady and anchoring long-term Profitability, even when the pace of litigation threatened to drag us down.

KPIs Across Pillars

Once we saw what KPIs could do for our Pipeline, we started wondering: What if we brought that same focus and clarity to the rest of our Set-Up?

In other words, if KPIs had worked so well with our Pipeline, surely, we could apply the same approach to each of our other core pillars: People, Process, and Product, and ultimately, Profitability.

Now, not only does the firm have quarterly KPIs (which apply to support staff), but individual lawyers set their own KPIs, as well.

Take the People pillar, for example. We wanted to build a reputation for leadership within the legal community. To make that goal real, one of our lawyers set a KPI to lead or teach two CLEs a year, actively contributing to knowledge-sharing within our field.

Another People KPI I've seen is to read one book on personal growth per quarter—a simple habit that strengthens both individual well-being and professional effectiveness.

Now, if you're wondering how People KPIs connect to financial outcomes, there's a direct link. Building a strong reputation leads to satisfied clients who refer us to others. KPIs in the People pillar keep our culture vibrant, helping us retain top talent, reduce turnover, and save money on recruitment and training. So, while it might not seem like a direct path from People KPIs to dollars in the bank, setting KPIs around People truly pays off in the long run.

When it comes to individual KPIs for the Pipeline, a lawyer might set goals outside of those the firm has set. It might be something like advancing a specific case from one stage in the Pipeline to the next within the quarter. Or they might decide to focus some time on networking with potential referral sources and set a KPI for how many contacts they make per quarter.

In terms of Process, a team member might take the initiative to design new or improved workflows, with a KPI to implement at least two workflow enhancements a year and track their impact on efficiency through metrics or time saved.

Under Product, we've seen KPIs such as crafting unique strategies for a client's case, measured by the case's ability to reach its Anticipated Value (as we discussed in chapter 4), and completing at least one focus group per quarter to refine case strategies. Additionally, one of our lawyers has tracked how many settlements meet our goal of policy limits offers, ensuring alignment with our strategic Objectives.

As for the firm, goals might include marketing objectives like increasing the number of cases we accept per month (Pipeline), completing four community service projects a year (People), or increasing the value of our book of business (Profitability). We've also set KPIs centered on receiving client feedback and increasing settlement values (Product).

To track our results from these efforts, we monitor client feedback through online reviews, track how many new clients come from referrals and which relationships are bringing them in, and keep an eye on social media mentions and engagement. We also track any awards and recognitions we receive, as these validate our standing in the legal community.

The right measurement doesn't just reflect progress—
it creates it.

This type of comprehensive strategy—engaging with KPIs across all aspects of our Set-Up—has fundamentally shifted our view of Profitability. It's no longer just an accidental outcome, but something we actively shape through our daily actions and strategic goals. Each quarter, as we set and meet our KPIs, we are building a more profitable and sustainable firm, with every metric moving us closer to our goals.

Set-Up Focus

Before I ever built a firm or started talking about Pipelines and KPIs, I was just a first-year law student. I'll never forget standing in the crowded hallway of the University of Oklahoma law school, staring at the white paper tacked to the wall. I was about to see something I'd never seen before.

There they were—three rows of eight-and-a-half-by-eleven-inch white sheets taped up for all to see, each labeled something like Torts I, Civ Pro, or Property. No names, just student ID numbers and final grades. I'd coasted through school my whole life, so I wasn't overly worried. But still, my stomach twisted as I slid my finger down the list.

Torts I: B+. Great. Civ Pro: B. Solid.

Then came Contracts: C−. Oof. That one stung. But the real hit came next.

Property I: D+. *Double take.*

Yep. Big, fat, black-felt-tip pen-un-freaking-believable D.

Plus.

I remember just staring at it. Not my best moment. My knees went a little weak. My chest got hot. My brain did that spiral thing where you're suddenly questioning every life choice you've ever made. What am I even doing here? Who was I kidding?

I was used to trusting my gut. Doing just enough and letting instinct carry me. But this—this grade—was hard data. A measurement.

That D+ was brutal, but it gave me a turning point. I built a new way of studying. Broke things down. Got organized. Stuck to it.

I figured out what worked for me and did it over and over again. And you know what? I graduated in the top 15 percent of my class.

All because I measured. Adjusted. Improved.

That's what KPIs are for your firm. They're not judgment or shame. They're not here to call you out. They're here to show you where you are so you can figure out where to go next.

And you don't need to track everything. Please don't. Just start with one pillar. One pain point. One process that feels clunky or unclear. Set a goal. Give it a timeline. Track it—not obsessively, just with intention. Then keep going.

If it feels like one more thing on your already-too-full plate, remember: You're already tracking something. It might just be in your head, on your calendar, or showing up as that pit-in-your-stomach feeling. KPIs just give structure to what you already know and help you turn instinct into actual insight.

There are prompts and examples in The Set-Up workbook to help you get started. Don't wait for perfect. Just start. Something small, something real. Because sometimes, the right measurement doesn't just reflect progress—it creates it.

KPI Quick Start: Seven Simple Steps

1. ***Choose one area.*** Pipeline, Process, People—pick just one to start.
2. ***Spot a pain point.*** Where are things stalling or getting messy? That's your clue.
3. ***Set a clear goal.*** Tie it to an outcome that matters: faster case resolution, more consistent client updates, increased referrals.
4. ***Pick one behavior to track.*** Make it specific and actionable (e.g., number of follow-ups completed, average days to resolution, number of five-star reviews).

5 ***Keep it simple.*** Ask yourself: Can I influence this? Will this help me make a decision? Can I track it without adding work?

6 ***Choose your rhythm.*** Weekly, monthly, per case—whatever keeps it visible without becoming noise.

7 ***Start small.*** One KPI is enough to change everything if it's the right one.

Steal this to begin: Track the number of days from Intake to demand package. That one metric alone will show you bottlenecks and cash flow health.

Remember: Missing a KPI isn't failure. It's feedback. The whole point is to see what's really happening so you can adjust early.

15

Mastering the Money

Profit is not an event. Profit is a habit.
MIKE MICHALOWICZ, *Profit First*

THIS PAST SPRING, I had one of those quiet, almost boring moments that would've been a full-blown panic attack in another season of my life.

It was early April, and the numbers were dipping just like they always do this time of year. Settlements slow down between January and March. I know this. I've lived through it more times than I can count. But still, those months used to send me into a week-long, 24/7 tailspin. I'd go into survival mode, running numbers late at night, wondering which vendors we could put off just a little longer, checking my own savings to see if I had enough to float the firm.

But I did none of that.

I opened my laptop and pulled up our Pipeline dashboard. Every case was there, complete with Anticipated Value and Anticipated Settlement Date. I scanned for cases in Stage Three—the wrap-up stage once a case has settled—and spotted a few solid ones set to close in mid-May. *Okay. There's that.*

Then I logged into our bank's customer portal. We have seven accounts, and I knew exactly what needed to be covered between

April and mid-May. I shifted a little money into the operating account for a cushion—just enough to breathe easier—and closed the laptop.

That was it. Ten, maybe twenty minutes? No mental gymnastics. No emergency scrambling. No "should we hold on paying experts just in case?" Just calm confidence.

When the funds came in May, we moved the cushion money right back where it came from. Then I looked at the Pipeline again, compared it to our overhead for the year, and knew we were fine. Actually, we were better than fine. We were covered for the rest of the year, even if nothing else settled.

That moment might not sound dramatic. But if you've ever spent a sleepless night wondering whether the numbers would stretch far enough to keep the lights on—or pay your team without a loan from your dad—you know how different it is. That quiet moment felt like freedom.

Just know it took time to get here. And two things: visibility and structure.

You've already seen in chapter 4 how the Pipeline gives us a clear view of Anticipated Value and timing, which give us an idea of what revenue is expected to come in and when. But visibility alone isn't enough to pay the bills if you don't have a plan for *what* to do when the money arrives.

Enter Mike Michalowicz

When I first sat down to write this book—and especially this section on Profitability—I knew I wasn't here to teach a crash course in accounting.

I'm not going to walk you through choosing a business structure (though ours is a PLLC), managing IOLTAs, or mastering profit and loss statements. Those things matter, absolutely. And I strongly recommend getting familiar with them or hiring smart people who are. A good accountant and a solid bookkeeper are worth their weight in gold.

And I'd be doing you a disservice if I didn't say this: Put checks and balances in place around your firm's finances. Not because you're suspicious, but because you're smart. Basic things, like one person reconciling the bank statements while someone else signs off. Limit who can write checks or swipe the credit card. Make it just inconvenient enough to do something careless or unethical. I've just seen too many firms blindsided. Sometimes by trusted employees who've been in the firm for years. Sometimes by well-meaning people who just didn't know what they were doing. A few safeguards now will help you sleep better, knowing the money's where it's supposed to be.

What I am going to show you, though, is something just as foundational.

I discovered it during a stretch where our financial stress had hit a breaking point. We were handling mostly bad faith cases at the time, which meant long timelines—eighteen months, sometimes two years or more. Settlements came in bursts, followed by long dry stretches, and when money finally hit, the pressure landed all at once: pay vendors, cover overhead, hope it would last.

We wanted to grow, but we were afraid to invest. Even if we tried, we had no idea if we could afford the support staff to sustain it. And taxes? Let's just say guessing your way through tax season is not a strategy I recommend.

Then my friend Sarah told me about *Profit First: Transform Your Business from a Cash-Eating Monster to a Money-Making Machine* by Mike Michalowicz. Michalowicz is a bestselling author known for creating simple, practical systems that help small businesses grow sustainably.

The core idea of *Profit First* hit me immediately: Most businesses spend everything they take in and cross their fingers that something's left over to pay the owner or the firm. (*Been there*!)

Michalowicz flips that. When money comes in, you take profit first, before you pay anything else. You set up separate bank accounts for profit, owner's pay, taxes, and operating expenses, then divide every dollar between them based on percentages you choose. This way, instead of wondering where your money goes, you know exactly where it is and what it's for, which gives you discipline in managing your money.

It sounded easy enough, so we decided to try it. Anything to get our numbers under control!

Every dollar needs
an actual job.

How We Do It

Of course, like most contingency-fee firms, we couldn't just follow the Profit First method straight out of the book. The core concept worked, but we had to make adjustments to fit our reality.

First, we can't treat every dollar that comes in as income. A big chunk of it doesn't even belong to us—it belongs to the client. And you don't touch client funds. Period. If you've ever seen what happens when a firm mishandles its trust account, you know why that line is sacred.

Then there are case expenses. In contingency work, we front those costs—filing fees, medical records, experts, investigators, whatever it takes to move the case forward. When the case resolves, we're reimbursed. But that's not income either. That's just getting back what we've already spent. On the books, those are assets, not revenue.

So yes, *Profit First*'s "pay yourself first" idea still works. But for us, it means paying true profit first, not phantom dollars. So, we layered in a few extra steps to make sure we are dealing with real, usable numbers.

We worked with our bank to create seven separate accounts:

- trust
- case expense
- owner's compensation
- profit
- tax
- operating
- marketing

Each account has a specific job, and together they make sure we know where every dollar is going. Fortunately, both our bank and our accountant were already familiar with the Profit First method, so the set-up was pretty painless.

The first account, the trust account, serves as our IOLTA, where all the funds from the resolution of each case are initially deposited. From here, we handle the client's portion of the settlement, pay referral fees, and manage the attorney's fee.

Where the Money Goes

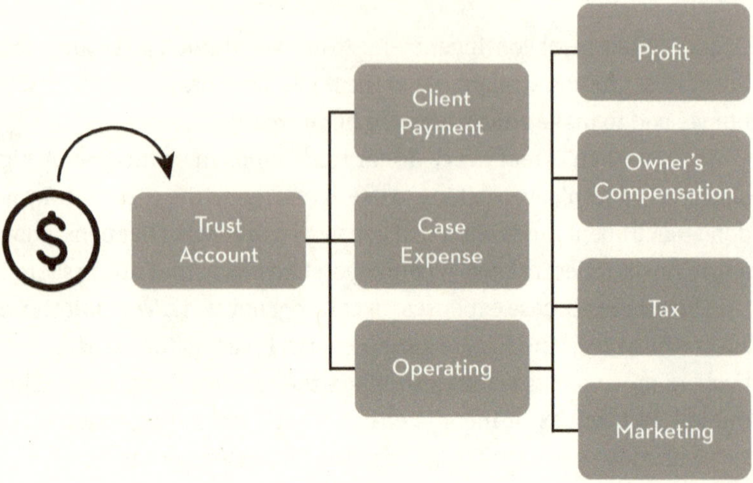

Here's how it breaks down with a $100,000 settlement:

- **Total Settlement Amount:** The entire $100,000 goes into our trust account.
- **Attorney's Fee:** One-third of the settlement, or $33,333, is allocated as the attorney's fee, which is transferred from the trust account to our operating account.
- **Referral Fee:** If a referring attorney is involved, 25 percent of the attorney's fee, or $8,333, is paid as a referral fee from the attorney's fee portion, leaving us $25,000 as our legal fee income (LFI).
- **Client's Portion:** The remaining two-thirds of the settlement, or $66,667, are designated as the client's portion.
- **Case Expense Reimbursement:** Case expenses are deducted from the client's portion. For example, if we fronted $10,000 in case expenses, this amount is reimbursed to our firm and transferred to our case expense account.
- **Client Payment:** After deducting case expenses, the remaining $56,667 is paid to the client from the trust account.

At this point, our firm's actual (gross) income from the case, our LFI, is $25,000. We take the LFI and allocate that across the remaining accounts.

- **Profit Account:** We started small—3 percent of LFI—and worked our way up to 10 percent. We increased a little each quarter until we hit our target. That reserve now helps us fund bonuses, reinvest in the firm, and breathe a little easier during leaner seasons.
- **Owner's Compensation:** We use the same gradual approach here. A percentage of LFI is set aside to pay Harrison and me. Before this system, we were often the last to get paid, if at all. We called it the hope-for-the-best compensation model. Highly motivating, not at all sustainable. Now, we know what's there.
- **Tax Account:** This was the one place we didn't ease into. From day one, we put 10 percent of LFI from each case into a dedicated tax account. We didn't want to scramble at the end of the year, or worse, come up short.
- **Marketing Account** (not originally part of our system, but important once we started working in personal injury): As the firm grew, we created a separate marketing reserve. Instead of allocating a percentage of LFI, we transfer a fixed amount each month based on our marketing plan. This way, we're investing in growth without pulling from operating.
- **Operating Account:** Whatever's left after funding the other accounts stays here. This covers payroll, rent, software, supplies, CLEs, and other day-to-day costs.

As you can see, each account has a purpose. And with the flexibility we've applied to our Profit First system, if we hit a short-term cash flow crunch, our operating account can "borrow" from profit or owner's compensation, but never from trust, case expense, or tax. We always immediately pay back the account we borrow from when new funds come in. This not only keeps us honest but helps maintain the firm's long-term priorities.

Where You Start

Now, I know that reading about a system and *starting* one are two different things. So, let's talk about how to get going wherever you are now.

If you bill by the hour, you likely have a relatively steady stream of revenue, even if it ebbs and flows with demand. Here's how to start:

1. Open a profit account and a tax account in addition to your operating account.
2. Pick a percentage—start with 1–5 percent of your gross revenue.
3. Every time you pay yourself or distribute funds, move those percentages into the designated accounts.

That's it. You're not changing your entire system; you're simply carving out space for structure.

If you collect lump sums up front, you're being paid now for work that may stretch over weeks or months. That means you need to *pace* the money. Here's one way to do that. When a payment comes in, immediately divide it across your accounts according to the percentages you've chosen, with the remainder going into your operating account:

- profit
- tax
- owner's compensation
- marketing

It's a good idea to create a client services reserve account to protect funds for long-term case work. This prevents the month-one spending spree that creates a month-three cash crunch.

If you're contingency-fee-based, you've seen how we do it. The main takeaway is not to treat the full settlement amount as income. It's not. Even after you've handled trust obligations, referral fees, and case expenses, you still must allocate your legal fee income to make sure you're covered where you need to be. Start with just 1–3 percent to profit. Build from there.

Real control over your money comes from structure—
not from obsessing over every penny.

In the end, it doesn't matter how you're paid—what matters is what you *do* with the money once it comes in. Profit First gives you a way to take control without having to track every penny. You'll know what you can spend, what you've saved, and what's already spoken for.

Then, once you've started, your only job is to stay consistent with your allocations and check in on your system at regular intervals. We do a full review of our allocations every month. That's when you ask yourself:

- Is the operating account running too tight?
- Are we growing, and do we want to raise the percentage on any of our accounts?
- Is the tax account overfunded (a good problem), and can we adjust slightly?
- Are we behind on owner's compensation, and if so, what needs to shift?

These reviews don't take long—maybe thirty minutes with a spreadsheet and your bookkeeper. But they make all the difference. Over time, we've adjusted our percentages upward, created a separate marketing reserve, and even added a buffer account for slow seasons.

You don't need to nail this from day one. Just set your starting numbers and commit to checking in and raising your percentages as you go. The system is designed to grow with you.

Set-Up Focus

Profit First and the Pipeline have been two of the most practical tools I've ever put in place. The Pipeline shows you what's coming in—the flow of cases and the revenue tied to them. Profit First makes sure that when that money lands, every dollar has a job. One gives you visibility; the other gives you intentional allocation. Together, they build the confidence that comes from knowing exactly where your firm stands. That's foundational.

"It just works," Harrison said one day about Profit First, almost offhand. "You set it and forget it. And for once, I'm not up at 2:00 a.m., doing math in my head." He's right. You're not constantly managing it because it's managing the essentials for you.

With the Pipeline giving you a clear view of what's coming in and Profit First mapping out where that money's going, you have an organized and predictable system and, as a result, calm.

Even better? When something's off—when the operating account feels tight, or a case hasn't moved—you don't have to dig through spreadsheets or scramble for answers. The system quietly flags the issue, giving insight into when to lean in and when to let it run.

And to be clear, this isn't about switching on autopilot and walking away. It's structure. Real structure, with built-in constraints—a discipline, as it were—that makes your financial decision-making easier. If there's not enough in the operating account, the answer is no. If the Pipeline doesn't show incoming revenue, you don't bank on hope; you make adjustments because you know exactly where you stand.

And with that, you've got each of your Set-Up pillars. Each pillar—People, Pipeline, Process, Product, Profitability—supports the other. They talk to each other. They nudge you toward the truth when something's off. Together, they give you more than just foundational strength. They give you a living, working strategy for running your entire firm.

the set-up

our strategy

WHEN I WAS IN seventh grade, all I wanted was to be like Dawn, the girl with the Trapper Keeper.

Dawn had it all—in the school supply department anyway. If you know, you know... the Trapper Keeper wasn't *just* a binder. It was this piece of genius, a godsend for the organized, and a distant dream for the rest of us.

Dawn's was this bright, neon yellow, and every time she opened it, you'd hear that glorious, attention-grabbing *r-r-r-rip* of Velcro. You'd swear it held the keys to seventh-grade success. And maybe it did. Her math homework, English essays, and some immaculate notes on physical science were all perfectly pristine.

She'd open up that thing, and there it was: her life. Everything arranged in perfect little folders, everything exactly where it was supposed to be. Calendars. Charts. A color-coded plan for every corner of her day.

Dawn was nothing like me. I was the type who just crumpled my assignments into the back of my spiral notebook, hoping to God they wouldn't fall out before I got home. Not exactly a blueprint for academic glory.

Fast forward a few (okay, nearly four) decades, and, in a twist no one saw coming—especially me—I'm the one with the structure, the color-coded sections, and the little place for every single thing. It's as if my firm's Set-Up has become my grown-up Trapper Keeper. It's organized, structured, reliable, and it's what keeps our work from flying off in a million directions.

People. Pipeline. Process. Product. Profitability. Each part has its own section, its own little universe, just like Dawn's folders. The People folder holds the heart. Pipeline propels the cases. Process is our how-to guide. Product is the polished work. And Profitability is that quiet pocket in the back that makes it all sustainable.

And you know, back then, I thought the Trapper Keeper itself was the magic. The bright colors, the Velcro, the way it looked in Dawn's hands. It felt like having one was the answer.

But now I get it. The real genius wasn't the binder itself; it was the *system* the binder gave you. The way it quietly held everything in place so you could focus on what mattered.

And that's the thing. When The Set-Up starts doing its quiet, behind-the-scenes work—when the pieces connect and start talking to each other—you get more than that gorgeous organization of the Trapper Keeper.

You get a firm that finally works like you always wanted it to. The overwhelm quiets. The mental load lifts. You're not scrambling every morning to put out fires because you're already ahead of them. Your team isn't looking to you for every answer; they're moving with clarity, because the path is built. The big questions—about money, growth, capacity—don't feel so foggy anymore. You're grounded in your Set-Up, knowing exactly where to look and what to do next.

That's where we're headed next: taking your Set-Up beyond the sum of its parts.

16

Beyond the Sum of Its Parts

We're all stories in the end. Just make it a good one, eh? Cause it was, you know. It was the best.
DOCTOR WHO, "The Big Bang"

WHEN YOU PICKED up this book, I'm guessing things weren't exactly serene at your firm. Maybe you'd hit that point where you thought something needed to change. Maybe someone who loves you handed you this book and said, "Here. Please. Read this before you implode." Whatever brought you here, I doubt everything was going perfectly and you were just looking for a little light reading.

And yet, here you are.

Whether you've already started putting pieces of The Set-Up into place or you're still sitting with the ideas, thinking about what they might mean for your firm, you've done something powerful. You've paused long enough to ask, "Is there a better way?" And my hope is that after seeing the pillars in full, you've come to the answer: "There is."

As you stick with it and The Set-Up truly takes hold—not as a checklist or a set of ideas, but as the quiet rhythm beneath how your firm runs—a kind of internal order begins to take root. It stops feeling like a tool you have to reach for and starts becoming the way you operate: how you lead, how your team moves, how decisions get made without second-guessing.

Bit by bit, you begin to trust the structure like you trust your own instincts. It becomes second nature. Not just something you *use* but something your firm is becoming.

That's when it really begins to show up in how you solve problems, how you grow with purpose, and how you stay steady when things get messy. Because once the system is part of you, it's not just keeping things running, but quietly moving you forward.

And really, wasn't that the hope when you turned that first page?

Diagnosis and Cure

When something goes wrong, it's easy to jump to conclusions, especially when you're under stress. A team member misses a deadline? It must be a motivation issue. Revenue dips? Time to blame marketing.

The Set-Up gives you a way to pause and look deeper. You can walk the problem through each pillar—People, Pipeline, Process, Product, and Profitability—and ask, "Where is this really breaking down?" That clarity turns snap judgment into focused decisions. And more often than not, what looks like one thing on the surface turns out to be something else entirely.

Let's say you've noticed your team is missing internal deadlines, clients are starting to get frustrated, and the work feels more chaotic than usual. At first, you might assume someone's just not doing their job. But walk it through The Set-Up's pillars, and you might find the real action to take is different.

People: You step back and notice the team feels disconnected, like they're just getting through tasks instead of believing in the work. The energy is off, and the mission feels distant.

Action: You bring values back into focus by telling a recent client story that reminds the team *why* this work matters, and you start making space to do it regularly.

Pipeline: When you look at your flow, it's not just the team; it's the system. Cases are stalling at the same stage again and again, and no one's quite sure who owns what.

Action: You review your Pipeline Objectives, clarify roles, and make sure each Objective is clearly assigned and consistently handled.

Process: Turns out, one of your Pipeline Objectives doesn't have a clear process behind it. People are improvising, and work gets dropped or repeated.

Action: You create a clear process with AI, define what "done" looks like, and make it visible so the team can follow it consistently.

Product: As disorganization increases, clients are starting to feel it. Calls are going unanswered. Updates are getting missed.

Action: You recommit to service standards and bring the client experience back into focus.

Profitability: Underneath it all, the lack of structure is creating waste. Team members are duplicating work, and delays are pushing costs up.

Action: You review your expenses, clean up KPIs, and make sure your pricing reflects the complexity of your cases.

Can you now see that what looked like a performance issue was actually a system issue, one you wouldn't have spotted without The Set-Up? That's the point. When you use it to diagnose, you stop throwing energy at symptoms and start fixing what's really broken.

Here's another common example: Revenue's down, your team is stretched, and the whole firm feels off. The knee-jerk reaction might be to turn up marketing, take more cases, or work harder. But when you step back and run the issue through your five pillars, the picture shifts.

Maybe the real issue is that the Pipeline is jammed. Or the Process is unclear. Or your Product has become inconsistent. Profitability is just the signal your system is showing you when something's out of alignment.

The Set-Up sharpens your thinking. It helps you spot what's off, focus your energy where it matters most, and move forward with clarity instead of spinning in circles. That's the power of using The Set-Up as a true diagnostic system.

Strategic "Tactic" Filter

We've all been there, right? The endless stream of emails, the sales pitches, the promises of tools that will catapult your income into the multimillions. AI for client communications, new systems to boost revenue, and fancy software that promises to make your firm run like a well-oiled machine. The possibilities seem endless, and each one is more alluring than the last.

But you know what? There's no need to chase after every shiny new object that comes your way. With The Set-Up as your strategic filter, you have a lens to assess whether each new opportunity is truly a good fit for your firm. Simply step back and ask: Does this align with the five pillars of your firm—People, Pipeline, Process, Product, and Profitability?

Take a recent example from my firm. We were approached by a vendor offering an AI tool to help prepare client demands. At first glance, it seemed promising—fast, efficient, potentially game-changing. But before we jumped in, we ran it through our Set-Up.

First, we considered the People and Product pillars. Would this tool support our team and enhance the work they already do, or would it undermine the critical thinking and personal touch we bring to our clients' demands?

Next, we ran it through the Pipeline and Process pillars. Would this tool improve our operational efficiency, or would it complicate an already well-oiled machine? Would it add value to our workflow, or just introduce another layer of technology that didn't truly fit?

When something's not working, slow down and walk it through each pillar with curiosity, not blame.

Going through these questions, we realized that no tool, however efficient, could replace the human element of our work. So, we decided to pass on it.

Now think about your own firm. Have you ever received a pitch that sounded almost too good to be true? A new platform. A clever app. A shortcut to growth. Before you dive in, try this: Pause and run it through your Set-Up.

People: Will this support your team or overwhelm them? Will it enhance your culture or introduce confusion?

Pipeline: Will it help cases move more smoothly through your Pipeline or create a bottleneck, or worse, a detour?

Process: Does it clarify how work gets done or make things more complicated? Will it improve consistency or add steps that don't belong?

Product: Will it make your service better, your outcomes stronger, your client experience sharper, or is it just noise dressed up as innovation?

Profitability: Will it save time? Protect your bottom line? Increase value over time? Or will it cost more in energy, money, and focus than it returns?

Even simple decisions—like signing up for a CLE—can benefit from this filter. Does it enhance your Product? Does it serve your Profitability? If not, it's okay to skip it.

Every opportunity sounds exciting at first. But not every opportunity deserves a yes. The Set-Up helps you say yes to what matters—what moves your firm forward—and no to what doesn't.

Scalability

Scalability. It's something that sounds big and complicated, like something only large firms need to worry about. But really, scalability is just about growth, and it's something you can count on The Set-Up to support, no matter the size of your firm.

How? It ensures that, as your firm grows, your foundation stays intact.

Whether you're adding cases, expanding your team, or launching new services, The Set-Up keeps your foundation intact—your systems, your values, and the direction you're heading. It evolves with your firm, so growth doesn't derail your progress.

Let's look at how that works, pillar by pillar:

People: Growth starts with leadership. As your firm expands, your role shifts and, with it, the emotional climate.

- Are you leading with the same clarity and calm that got you here?
- Is your culture strong enough to scale?
- Are your values being reinforced or watered down as new people come in?

Focus: As you grow, doubling down on culture and communication becomes essential. Reaffirm your values often. Model the leadership your team needs. Create rituals that keep your mission alive, even as the firm gets bigger.

Pipeline: More cases don't mean more chaos if your flow is solid.

- Are your stages still serving your needs as volume increases?
- Do you need new Roles or Objectives to handle the volume?
- Are bottlenecks forming where there used to be flow?

Focus: You may need to add stages, refine handoffs, or rebalance workloads, but your Pipeline keeps the system from breaking down.

Process: With more clients comes more complexity, unless your systems are strong.

- Are key steps still clear and consistently followed?
- Are team members improvising instead of executing?
- Is your Process keeping pace with your growth?

Focus: Scaling doesn't mean adding more steps. It means shaping your Process so your team can do the work with confidence and calm, even as the pace picks up.

Product: Growth should never dilute the quality of what you deliver.

- Is client experience still consistent across the board?
- Has quality slipped as caseload increased?
- Are new team members delivering at the level you expect?

Focus: Use The Set-Up to keep your standards high, your training tight, and your client experience intentional, even as you expand.

Profitability: Revenue doesn't mean much if you're not keeping enough of it.

- Is your pricing still aligned with your costs and capacity?
- Are expenses creeping up in ways you didn't anticipate?
- Is inefficiency eating into your profit?

Focus: Growth without profitability is just busyness. The Set-Up helps you keep your eye on the numbers and make smarter decisions.

The beauty of The Set-Up is that it doesn't fight growth. It supports it. As your firm expands, this framework helps you scale intentionally, without losing control of what matters most.

Legacy

As I think about the journey we've been on and everything we've built, I feel good about the future of my firm, even knowing that one day, my role in it will change. I'll step back, slowly at first, then maybe more fully. And while that thought is bittersweet, it's also comforting.

That's the gift of The Set-Up. It builds something bigger than you. I see it now in small moments: when a team member handles a difficult client situation using our values as their guide, when another team member makes a strategic decision that perfectly aligns with our Pipeline thinking even though we never discussed that specific scenario, or when someone new joins and quickly absorbs not just our Set-Up but the *why* behind it.

That's when you know The Set-Up has become more than a system you implemented. It's become the way your people think, the lens through which they see problems and solutions.

And that's what gives you space to step back. Because when something is this deeply woven into your firm's DNA, transitions don't feel like the big, scary thing they used to be. The culture, the workflows, the everyday decisions aren't dependent on any one person. They're just part of how the team functions.

So, when you're ready to hand over the reins, it doesn't feel like you're walking out and leaving your team behind. They're ready. Because The Set-Up is something that outlasts any individual founder.

Taking the Firm's Temperature

Even with a strong foundation, you still need to check the pulse. For me, that habit started long before I ever ran a law firm.

I didn't set out to develop my November ritual. Not at all. It just kind of happened back in college, probably as my way of staving off the feeling I was hurtling through life, slightly out of control.

You probably remember how college feels. It's like trying to drink from a fire hose, with everything coming at you so fast. Classes, exams, midnight pizza runs with friends you're sure you'll stay close to forever. Amid all that frenzy, one November day I looked up and thought, "Who's running this show? Are you really doing okay? Is this what you want?" And, maybe most importantly, "Are you still you in there?" So, I sat myself down, like the benevolent but steady boss of "me," and took stock.

Nothing formal, really. Not at first. Just a moment of trying to get the car pointed in the right direction. And by some miracle, it helped. It gave me a tiny sense of calm, a little clarity in the midst of the noise. I could breathe a bit easier, knowing I had checked in with myself.

Then I did it the next November. And the one after that. I started referring to it as "taking my life's temperature." And it became this cozy, secret ritual, like writing little notes to my future self, reminding me to stay awake and aware. It followed me into my grown-up life, through my years of teaching, and then going to law school, where things just got busier and busier.

But still, this November thing stuck around.

Until it didn't.

Somewhere in those early years of lawyering, diaper-changing, and running on fumes, I just stopped. Not by conscious choice, really. It just sort of quit happening. And with that, I was no longer checking in with myself. I must have been giving myself the silent treatment, because without even realizing it, I lost track of "me" in the whole process of showing up for everyone else.

Then came that drive to Texarkana, which, if you recall, was my first real "Wait a second, I have a say in this" moment. That drive cracked something open in me, and from then on, I decided to reclaim a little part of myself. And wouldn't you know it? Back came the November ritual. Except this time, it was different. I didn't just need it for me. I needed it for my firm.

Every November now, I sit down and take the firm's temperature. I ask the same questions I once asked myself: "Are we healthy? Are we pointed in the right direction? Are we really doing what we set out to do?"

This is where the structure of The Set-Up is so powerful an asset. I use it to examine every nook and cranny of the firm. Is our Process still working? Are our People supported? Do we have enough financial resilience?

Taking the firm's temperature has become one of the most grounding parts of my year. It's like calling a time-out, pausing to figure out where to focus, set specific goals for each pillar, and make sure our daily work still reflects the mission we set out to serve.

I strongly recommend you begin your own yearly check-in. You don't have to do it in November like me, but you do need to plan for it. Block off half a day—or even a full day—and give yourself space for real reflection. Invite your partners or key team members so the work doesn't fall on your shoulders alone.

This isn't something to rush. Set a steady pace, take breaks, and let it be a meaningful time to look at the big picture of your Set-Up and the

Every opportunity sounds exciting at first. But not every opportunity deserves a yes.

smaller systems that keep things running. You'll be asking: "What's working? Where do we need to grow? And what's ready for a reset?"

If you want a full walkthrough of what that check-in can look like, complete with guided questions and KPIs for each pillar of The Set-Up, you'll find it all waiting for you in The Set-Up workbook. But here's the most important thing: Don't skip the pause. Whether it's once a year or once a quarter, give yourself the gift of stepping back and looking honestly at the whole picture.

That's how you keep The Set-Up not just in place, but alive.

Set-Up Focus

AJ Harper, a brilliant writer and Mike Michalowicz's longtime collaborator, uses a metaphor for authorship she calls the "six-lane highway."

Being an author, she says, is like driving on a highway with six lanes—each one with its own purpose, each leading somewhere important. There's a lane for writing, of course, but also for marketing, building your platform, planning for publication, and maybe even drafting a proposal to catch someone's interest.

The trick is learning how to switch lanes. Sometimes, you need to stay focused in one for a while, pouring all your energy into it. Other times, you have to shift quickly from writing to logistics, from platform-building to long-range planning.

It's not always easy, and it can feel a little chaotic. But it works—because every lane has a role. The key is trusting that even when you're switching lanes a lot, you're still making progress. You're still moving forward. And you're keeping your hands on the wheel without spinning off the road, knowing all those lanes will eventually take you where you want to go.

I absolutely love this metaphor. Because, like authorship, building and running a firm isn't about staying in one lane, even if staying in one might feel easier. Each pillar of The Set-Up has its own lane:

- *People* is where you lead and shape culture.
- *Pipeline* structures your workflow.
- *Process* ensures your "how" is clear.
- *Product* centers your clients through best practices.
- *Profitability* monitors the health of it all.
- *The Set-Up* is your strategy lane—the system that integrates and aligns all the others.

Sometimes you'll be deep in one lane, giving it your full attention. Other times, you'll shift between lanes, making sure they stay aligned as you move forward. The Set-Up gives you the framework to do that. It makes those transitions smoother and more intentional, so you don't lose sight of the big picture.

So, think of your firm as your own six-lane highway. No matter which lane you're in, you're not sitting still. The Set-Up keeps you steady, lets you shift with purpose, and ensures every part of your business moves forward, always aligned with where you want to go.

17

The Next Chapter Is Yours

Dreams don't have deadlines.

LL COOL J

OVER TEN YEARS AGO when I started my firm, I dreamed of building something that mattered—something successful, meaningful, and uniquely *ours*. But there was no guidebook. No roadmap with clear directions, saying, "Here's how to do it. Here's what works, and here's what doesn't." It was incredibly frustrating.

I knew I had the freedom to create whatever I wanted. No one was standing in my way. But freedom without direction is overwhelming. And as I've shared, I spent years figuring it out through trial and error. Some things worked beautifully. Others, not really. It was a journey full of missteps and small wins that slowly added up.

But it doesn't have to be that way for you.

That's why I wrote this book... for you. So you don't have to go through the same painful process I did, struggling to find your way through it all. I mean this book to be the guide I wish I'd had, built from everything I learned the hard way.

Of course, just like when I started the firm, when I decided to start writing, I thought, "How hard can it be?" I'd been preparing legal briefs for three decades, after all! So, I dove in, pouring out what I thought was everything about The Set-Up in just a few months.

But something was missing. I could feel it, even as I typed the final sentences. I had words on paper, but they were just words. It didn't feel quite right.

As it turns out, writing a book to help others is a completely different animal from writing briefs for judges. *Completely.*

The truth is that first draft was rough. Extremely, painfully rough. Author Anne Lamott would call it a "shitty first draft." *Indeed.* It read more like a textbook—a dry, lifeless guide I'm pretty sure even *I* wouldn't want to read.

I knew in my gut something was missing. But I didn't know how to fix it.

That's when I got my first nudge—an email from the guy who had saved us with his book *Profit First.* But I'll be honest—sorry, Mr. Michalowicz—I don't always read his emails. But this one grabbed me. The subject line: Don't Write That Book.

Was the universe trying to tell me something?

You know me by now. I'm stubborn. So... I ignored it.

A couple of weeks later, the second nudge came in the form of the same email from Michalowicz: *Don't Write That Book.*

Ugh! But I need to write that book!

This time, my better angels took hold, and I caved. I opened it.

Inside, he described a podcast he was doing with his writing partner, AJ Harper, about writing books meant to help others. *That's what I was trying to do!* Intrigued, I gave it a listen. And wow! They were speaking directly to me.

I binged that podcast like a Netflix series. Then I ordered Harper's book, *Write a Must-Read,* and pored over it, highlighting and writing notes in the margins just like I did in law school. Everything she said made sense. My first draft wasn't enough. Not if I truly wanted to help you.

But knowing I needed to fix the book and actually doing it were two different things. I had to unlearn thirty years of legal writing habits and completely shift how I approached this project. It was hard!

Your dream is still alive. No matter how long it's taken, whatever detours you've faced, it's there, waiting for your next step.

But that's where the gift of AJ Harper and her team, Laura and Sade, saved me. Over the next several months, I devoured what they had to teach me in an editing workshop and daily writing sprints. I was even fortunate enough to attend Harper's writing retreat on Madeline Island in Wisconsin—a magical place where I met five other authors also on a journey of writing books meant to help others.

We worked. We laughed. We cried. And we rewrote. It was life-changing. Book-changing.

More than anything else, it opened my eyes to what this book could be for you—a resource that truly serves you, the reader. It wasn't about me anymore at all. It was about helping *you* transform your firm.

In many ways, this mirrors the journey you've been on throughout this book. Perhaps when you started, you were filled with chaos, frustration, even a little self-doubt. You worked through The Set-Up, pillar by pillar, learning what works and what doesn't.

My hope for you is that now you have clarity. You're seeing your firm in a whole new way. You're empowered to take control of your firm, knowing exactly how to make it work. You can now make better decisions and build something truly extraordinary.

Sure, your firm might have felt like your own "shitty first draft" at the start—no offense—but that's just where transformation begins. Look at what you've built so far with your Set-Up. It's refined, intentional, and aligned with your vision.

So, my final thought for you as we close is simple: You're ready for this. You're that same person who had a spark of innovation that inspired you to start a firm or take one over. You've done the hard things, and you've got a plan to keep moving.

I mean, if I could go from a trial-and-error firm owner to someone who confidently runs a thriving practice, so can you. If I could transform my first draft of this book into something meaningful and truly helpful, you can transform your firm into something extraordinary.

The understanding, the empowerment, the confidence—it's all yours for the taking. You've already done the hard work by showing up, reading this book, and putting your Set-Up into action. Now, take what you've built and run with it.

This isn't the end of your journey. No matter how long it's taken or how many detours you've faced, your dream is still alive, waiting for you to take the next step. The work you've done, the clarity you've gained—it's all fuel for the future you've envisioned.

In the words of the OG of reinvention himself—Mr. LL Cool J—"Dreams don't have deadlines." They don't expire. They don't run out of time. They're always there, ready for you to bring them to life.

So, keep your Set-Up nearby. Revisit it often. Let it grow with you.

The next chapter is yours to write.

And know I'll be right here, cheering you on every step of the way.

Acknowledgments

BOOKS MAY have one name on the cover, but as Anne Lamott says, no one writes alone. (Okay, that might not be an exact quote, but she'd agree.) This one was built by a whole community who believed in me when I wasn't sure I could pull it off.

To my husband, Mark—you lived every doubt with me. You sat through the nights when I stared at the screen wondering if I had anything worth saying and told me to keep going anyway. You steadied me through every high and low of this wild ride, and you never once flinched when I shoved another half-baked chapter your way and said, "Does this even make sense?" You let me read the words out loud until they finally sounded like truth, and more of you is in these pages than anyone will ever know. You helped me see things clearer, reach a little higher, and believe this could be more than just a good idea.

To Alex and Delaney—you are the reason any of this exists. Truly. Being your mom has always been the only job in the world I ever really wanted. Everything else—even my firm—was just a way to try and make room for that. *You're* why it matters. *You're* why I can tell every reader The Set-Up can give them a different kind of life—because I built it to save ours, and it did. (Oh, and thank you for keeping me from sounding like a hopeless Gen Xer in those early drafts!)

To Harrison—you believed in what I wanted to build from day one. You've been here through every up and down, twist and turn. I'll never forget that day in my sunroom when we signed our first partnership agreement. "We're married now," we said, knowing the enormity of it all and that our lives were about to change. You didn't just stick with me—you helped build this. Thank you for helping me figure out how to make plan A work.

To my team—you've already got the dedication, but you deserve a second thank-you here. You carried the weight of the firm so I could pour into this book. You lived out The Set-Up every day and gave me the courage to put our story into words. You also saw the doubts, the pivots, the messy middle and kept believing in this work right alongside me. You bless me beyond measure. And to the Sill team—thank you for walking alongside us on our shared journey. Better together, always.

To Gene, my very first business coach, and to Sarah S., Sarah B., Sara Jane, Jill, Laura, Claire, Joni, and Peter—your voices were the ones I heard in the dark, back when starting the firm felt like stepping off a cliff. Remember, sitting with me on my living room floor, asking the hard questions, and holding the hope I couldn't quite hold myself. You gave me the courage to take the leap and the safety net to believe I wouldn't fall. Everything I've built traces back to that circle. I've been building on it ever since.

To every lawyer who let me test the Pipeline and other parts of this book inside your own firms over the years—thank you for trusting me. Your willingness to experiment and try a new way of working gave me proof that this framework could change more than just my own firm.

Before any of this ever existed—even the shadow of an idea of it—there was Catherine Burnett, my high school English teacher, who taught me structure and all the little rules that still run under every sentence I write. Just like *The Set-Up* is about building your firm on a solid foundation, Ms. Burnett gave me the foundation so I could write about it.

To Shannon Butler and Rick Hadrava—you were the first to say, "You can do this." Shannon, you pushed. Rick, you told me to 10X. You refused to let me think small. You were the first brave souls to read the "shitty first draft" and believed there was something worth saving.

To AJ Harper—you didn't just teach me how to write a book that serves the reader; you modeled what it looks like to turn a book into a business without ever losing your integrity. You walked me through the fear of unlearning thirty years of legal writing habits and reminded me that a book is forever, so I better make it a good one. You, Laura, and Sade, along with every friend in the T3 community, made sure I never had to navigate this roller coaster alone. And AJ, I'll never forget you and Polly opening up your beautiful lake house to us—that was the first time I could say out loud, with any confidence at all, that I was an author. My writing—and my life—has been forever changed.

To my advanced readers—you said yes to holding an unfinished book and trusted me enough to give your honest feedback. You caught the rough edges, celebrated what was working, and helped me shape this into something stronger and clearer. Your early encouragement gave me the fuel to keep going when the finish line still felt far away.

To my Page Two partners—Jesse, Tass, Sheila, Beth, Raya, Fiona, Kendra, Peter, and all the rest—thank you for turning a too-long and messy draft into a book I'm proud to put into the world. From that very first Zoom call, Jesse, you just got it. You gave me more encouragement and confidence than you'll ever know, and that carried me all the way through. Your guidance, patience, and expertise didn't just get this project across the finish line, you made me believe it belonged there.

And to my mom, my dad, my sisters, Cindy, Amy, Elizabeth, and every other friend and quiet encourager who asked, "How's the book going?" or told me to keep going when I wasn't sure I could: You are part of these pages, too.

Finally, to you, the reader. This book is yours now. Take it, use it, make it your own.

Notes

Chapter 1: It Wasn't Supposed to Be This Hard

p. 5 *"Unless someone like you cares a whole awful lot":* Dr. Seuss, *The Lorax* (Random House, 1971).

p. 6 *About 20 percent of new businesses don't make it past the first two years:* Chart 3, "Business Employment Dynamics: Entrepreneurship and the U.S. Economy," US Bureau of Labor Statistics, last modified September 28, 2023, bls.gov/bdm/entrepreneurship/bdm_chart3.htm.

Chapter 2: Shifting Perspective

p. 17 *"Change. But start slowly":* Edson Marques, *Mude* (Panda Books, 2005).

Chapter 3: A New Way to Work the Work

p. 33 *"You wanna fly":* Toni Morrison, *Song of Solomon* (Alfred A. Knopf, 1977).

Chapter 4: What Happens When the Work Works

p. 55 *"Life moves pretty fast": Ferris Bueller's Day Off,* written and directed by John Hughes, featuring Matthew Broderick (Paramount Pictures, 1986).

p. 61 *75 percent of people with high role clarity say they're happier at work:* Lieke Pijnacker, "HR Analytics: Role Clarity Impacts Performance," *Effectory*, September 25, 2019, effectory.com/knowledge/hr-analytics-role-clarity-impacts-performance/.

p. 64 *When accountability is shared by everyone, workflows run more smoothly:* Maarten Renkema, Tanya Bondarouk, and Anna Bos-Nehles, "Transformation to Self-Managing Teams: Lessons

Learned: A Look at Current Trends and Data," *Strategic HR Review* 17, no. 2 (2018): 81–84, doi.org/10.1108/SHR-10-2017-0072.

Chapter 5: It All Depends on You

p. 79 *"Not everything that is faced can be changed":* James Baldwin, "As Much Truth as One Can Bear," *The New York Times Book Review* (January 14, 1962); James Baldwin, *The Cross of Redemption: Uncollected Writings*, ed. Randall Kenan (Vintage International, 2011).

p. 80 *An organization's ability to succeed is limited by its leader's ability to lead:* John C. Maxwell, "Law of the Lid," *Maxwell Leadership® Blog*, July 19, 2013, johnmaxwell.com/blog/the-law-of-the-lid/.

p. 85 *Your firm's climate has a huge impact on your bottom line:* Daniel Goleman, "Leadership That Gets Results," *Harvard Business Review*, 78, no. 2 (March–April 2000): 78–90.

p. 86 *These are research-backed markers that reveal:* Goleman, "Leadership That Gets Results," 78–90.

Chapter 6: What Kind of Leader Are You, Really?

p. 89 *"There is nothing noble in being superior":* W.L. Sheldon, "What to Believe: An Ethical Creed," *Ethical Addresses* 4, no. 4 (April 1897): 61. See full discussion on this quote at quoteinvestigator.com/2017/03/11/superior/.

p. 89 *Self-awareness, after all, is the cornerstone of effective leadership:* Paola Cecchi-Dimeglio, "How Self-Awareness Elevates Leadership Effectiveness," *Forbes*, February 14, 2024, forbes.com/sites/paolacecchi-dimeglio/2024/02/14/how-self-awareness-elevates-leadership-effectiveness/.

p. 98 *The best leaders serve first:* Robert L. Greenleaf, *The Servant as Leader* (Greenleaf Center for Servant Leadership, 2008).

p. 98 *"A leader is like a shepherd":* Nelson Mandela, *Long Walk to Freedom: The Autobiography of Nelson Mandela* (Little, Brown, 1994).

p. 98 *"The heart of leadership is putting others ahead of yourself":* John C. Maxwell, *The 21 Irrefutable Laws of Leadership: Follow Them and People Will Follow You* (Thomas Nelson, 1998).

p. 99 *"I was always a transactional leader":* Mike Miliard, "Nick Saban Offers Some Valuable Lessons on Leadership," *Healthcare IT News*, March 18, 2024, healthcareitnews.com/news/nick-saban-offers-some-valuable-lessons-leadership.

p. 102 *"A good leader remains focused":* John C. Maxwell, "Law of Navigation," *The 21 Irrefutable Laws of Leadership: Follow Them and People Will Follow You* (Thomas Nelson, 1998).

Chapter 7: The Practice of Phenomenal Leadership

p. 107 *"The journey is the reward":* Andy Hertzfeld, "Credit Where Due," Folklore.org, January 1983, folklore.org/Credit_Where_Due.html.

Chapter 8: What Is Your "Why"?

p. 115 *"Your work is to find out what your work should be": The Dhammapada,* v. 166, ed. Anne Bancroft (Vega Books, 2003).

p. 121 *Companies with a strong sense of purpose consistently outperform their peers:* Claudine Gartenberg, Andrea Prat, and George Serafeim, "Corporate Purpose and Financial Performance," *Organization Science* 30, no. 1 (January–February 2019): 1–18, doi.org/10.2139/ssrn.2840005.

p. 121 *When employees feel connected to a firm's mission, they're more productive:* "State of the American Workplace," Gallup, last updated 2017, gallup.com/workplace/238085/state-american-workplace-report-2017.aspx.

p. 121 *Purpose-oriented employees are 54 percent more likely to stay:* Aaron Hurst, Adam Pearce, Cammie Erickson, et al., *Purpose at Work: The 2016 Global Report* (LinkedIn and Imperative, 2016).

Chapter 9: Putting Your Why Into Action

p. 129 *"Don't say things. What you are stands over you":* Ralph Waldo Emerson, *Letters and Social Aims* (James R. Osgood, 1876), 85.

p. 132 *"A value is a way of being or believing":* Brené Brown, *Dare to Lead: Brave Work. Tough Conversations. Whole Hearts* (Random House, 2018), 186.

p. 135 *"Anything less than a conscious commitment to the important":* Stephen R. Covey, *The 7 Habits of Highly Effective People* (Free Press, 1989).

p. 136 *The idea of a quick daily team huddle:* Verne Harnish, *Mastering the Rockefeller Habits: What You Must Do to Increase the Value of Your Growing Firm* (Gazelles, 2002); Verne Harnish, *Scaling Up: How a Few Companies Make It . . . and Why the Rest Don't* (Gazelles, 2022).

Process—Our Engine

p. 149 *"The details are not the details": ECS,* short, featuring Charles Eames (Herman Miller, 1961); Eames Demetrios, *An Eames Primer* (Universe Publishing, 2001), 172.

Chapter 10: The Invisible Engine

p. 151 *"The most difficult thing is the decision to act":* Amelia Earhart, *Last Flight*, ed. George Palmer Putnam (Harcourt, Brace, 1937).

p. 157 *"The system runs the business":* Michael E Gerber, *The E-Myth Revisited: Why Most Small Businesses Don't Work and What to Do About It* (Harper Business, 1995).

p. 158 *To regain focus after even a small interruption:* Kermit Pattison, "Worker, Interrupted: The Cost of Task Switching," *Fast Company*, July 12, 2008, fastcompany.com/944128/worker-interrupted-cost-task-switching.

p. 161 *Hundreds of millions of workers may need to shift careers:* James Manyika, Susan Lund, Michael Chui, et al., *Jobs Lost, Jobs Gained: Workforce Transitions in a Time of Automation*, McKinsey Global Institute (McKinsey, December 2017).

Chapter 11: It's All About the Client

p. 173 *"The simple act of paying attention":* Keanu Reeves, *What Keanu Says: The Unofficial Collection* (Quadrille, 2025).

p. 174 *The better you understand what drives your client:* Stephen Ellmann, "Lawyers and Clients Symposium: Clinical Education," *UCLA Law Review* 34, no. 3 (1986): 717–79.

p. 175 *Jacob was doing:* active listening: *Active Listening:* Carl R. Rogers, *Client-Centered Therapy: Its Current Practice, Implications, and Theory* (Houghton Mifflin, 1951).

p. 186 *Where the lasting fulfillment in this work comes from:* Research in self-determination tells us that we experience greater fulfillment when our work satisfies core psychological needs, including a sense of meaningful connection to others. See Edward L. Deci and Richard M. Ryan, "The 'What' and 'Why' of Goal Pursuits: Human Needs and the Self-Determination of Behavior," *Psychological Inquiry* 11, no. 4 (2000): 227–68.

p. 186 *"People will never forget how you made them feel":* Maya Angelou, *Wouldn't Take Nothing for My Journey Now* (Bantam Books, 1993).

Chapter 12: A Better Way to Serve

p. 187 *"Victorious warriors win first and then go to war":* Sun Tzu, *The Art of War*, trans. Samuel B. Griffith (Oxford University Press, 1963).

Profitability—Our Results

p. 202 *We adopted Profit First principles:* Profit First® is a financial strategy developed by Mike Michalowicz. For more on his method, visit mikemichalowicz.com. See Mike Michalowicz, *Profit First: Transform Your Business from a Cash-Eating Monster to a Money-Making Machine* (Portfolio, 2017).

Chapter 13: Investing in People

p. 203 *"My Precious":* J.R.R. Tolkien, "A Long-Expected Party," *The Fellowship of the Ring* (Houghton Mifflin, 1954).

p. 204 *Highly engaged teams see a 21 percent increase in profits:* Jim Harter, "Employee Engagement on the Rise in the US," *News: Economy*, Gallup, August 26, 2018, news.gallup.com/poll/241649/employee-engagement-rise.aspx.

p. 204 *Companies that prioritize the employee experience are four times more profitable:* Jason Flynn, Sue Cantrell, David Mallon, Lauren Kirby, and Nicole Scoble-Williams, "The Transparency Paradox: Could Less Be More When It Comes to Trust?" in *2024 Global Human Capital Trends* (Deloitte Insights, 2024), 43. See deloitte.com/content/dam/insights/articles/glob176836_global-human-capital-trends-2024/DI_Global-Human-Capital-Trends-2024.pdf.

p. 204 *The "secret sauce" for business success:* Jacqueline Brassey, Aaron De Smet, Emily Field, et al., "To Defend Against Disruption, Build a Thriving Workforce," *Our Insights*, McKinsey Global Institute, May 8, 2024, mckinsey.com/capabilities/people-and-organizational-performance/our-insights/to-defend-against-disruption-build-a-thriving-workforce.

p. 207 *The real path to results isn't nonstop hustle:* Cal Newport, *Slow Productivity: The Lost Art of Accomplishment Without Burnout* (Portfolio, 2024).

p. 207 *Companies offering true flexibility see higher engagement:* Jennifer Moss, "Creating a Happier Workplace Is Possible—and Worth It," *Harvard Business Review*, updated November 7, 2023, hbr.org/2023/10/creating-a-happier-workplace-is-possible-and-worth-it.

p. 207 *When employees feel trusted:* Lonnie Golden, Julia Henly, and Susan Lambert, "Work Schedule Flexibility: A Contributor to Employee Happiness?," *Journal of Social Research and Policy*, December 2013, doi.org/10.2139/ssrn.2129520.

p. 210 *Replacing them can cost anywhere from* half to twice their salary: Shane McFeely and Ben Wigert, "This Fixable Problem Costs US Businesses $1 Trillion," *Workplace*, Gallup, March 13, 2019, gallup.com/workplace/247391/fixable-problem-costs-businesses-trillion.aspx.

Chapter 14: Measure It and It Will Come

p. 215 *"It is not enough to be busy":* Henry David Thoreau, *The Journal of Henry David Thoreau*, ed. Bradford Torrey and Francis H. Allen, vol. 9, 1856–1857 (Houghton Mifflin, 1906).

p. 216 *The measures that "tell management how the organization is performing":* David Parmenter, *Key Performance Indicators: Developing, Implementing, and Using Winning KPIs*, 4th ed. (Wiley, 2019), 4.

p. 217 *When your team knows exactly what's being tracked:* Christopher D. Ittner and David F. Larcker, "Coming Up Short on Non-Financial Performance Measurement," *Harvard Business Review* 81, no. 11 (November 2003): 88–95, hbr.org/2003/11/coming-up-short-on-nonfinancial-performance-measurement.

Chapter 15: Mastering the Money

p. 229 *"Profit is not an event":* Mike Michalowicz, *Profit First* (Portfolio, 2017).

Chapter 16: Beyond the Sum of Its Parts

p. 243 *"We're all stories in the end": Doctor Who*, episode 212b, "The Big Bang," written by Steven Moffat, directed by Toby Haynes, featuring Matt Smith, Karen Gillian, and Arthur Darvill, aired June 26, 2010, on BBC One.

Chapter 17: The Next Chapter Is Yours

p. 257 *"Dreams don't have deadlines":* LL Cool J, "LL Cool J Talks Upcoming Arena Tour, Festival," CBS Mornings, aired August 1, 2023, on CBS, cbs.com/shows/video/RsqEAEs1uTashlPODEKoCsdJMckwCcPH/.

p. 258 *"Shitty first draft":* Anne Lamott, *Bird by Bird: Some Instructions on Writing and Life* (Anchor, 1994), 20.

SHEVAUN WILLIAMS

About the Author

SIMONE FULMER GAUS is co-founder of Fulmer Sill, a nationally recognized law firm based in Oklahoma City, focusing on personal injury, bad faith, and mass torts.

After seventeen years in practice, Simone was done with burnout and business as usual in the traditional law firm setting. She believed there had to be a better way to run a law firm—one that didn't cost your soul to succeed. So, in 2014, she started her own firm to find out if it was possible.

That journey led to The Set-Up™, a new model for running a law firm with more focus, more heart, and a lot less noise. In the eleven years since, her firm's revenue has grown more than thirteen times, proving that you can thrive in this business without sacrificing yourself or your team in the process.

Simone lives in Oklahoma City with her husband, Mark, in a house run by three Doodles and two Ragdolls. They share four grown kids and have recently stepped into their favorite role yet: grandparents.

Why Stop Now?

If *The Set-Up* became that "elbow in your pocket" you've needed and gave you the inspiration to perfect your swing, don't let that momentum fade into good intentions.

Build It. Fix It. Make It Work.

The Set-Up gives you the strategy, and its companion workbook walks you through implementation. It's your guide for putting the pillars into action based on your firm's unique structure, needs, and goals.

The workbook meets you where you are and walks you through the real work of building a better firm, whether you're building from scratch, fixing what's not working, or fine-tuning as you grow.

Available at your favorite online retailer. Bulk team pricing is available at theset-up.co.

Bonus Content, Anyone?

I started this book with 87,000 words and cut it down to 65,000. Some great case studies and practical examples didn't make it into the final version. But they're too good to waste. Grab your reader-exclusive bonus content at theset-up.co/bonuscontent.

Ready to Go Deeper?

I work directly with a small number of firm owners each year—leaders serious about transformation and ready to move beyond quick fixes. If you want a strategic partner to guide you in building a sustainable practice, let's talk.

Bringing The Set-Up to You

I also speak at CLEs, industry events, and on podcasts, sharing insights on the following:

- leadership and team alignment
- role clarity
- burnout prevention
- sustainable firm growth

My goal is always to leave the audience with ideas they can use right away and the energy to act on them.

Find out more at theset-up.co/speaking.

Don't Miss What's Next

Join my email list for updates, free tools, and new resources to help you build your own Set-Up. I also have some exciting offerings in the works for those who want to help others in implementing their Set-Up. Stay tuned.

Join at theset-up.co.

One Last Thing

If this book helped you, please take a moment to leave a review. Just a few honest sentences on your favorite bookseller's site can be the nudge another firm owner needs to avoid years of trial and error.

Thanks again for joining me. I can't wait to see what you build!

www.ingramcontent.com/pod-product-compliance
Lightning Source LLC
LaVergne TN
LVHW100258210926
848480LV00003B/958
* 9 7 8 1 7 7 4 5 8 6 9 3 8 *